WHAT'S IN EMERALD CITY?
THE POWER OF THE HEART

WHAT'S IN EMERALD CITY?
THE POWER OF THE HEART

A Memoir of Trauma and Survival

YOLANDA TREVINO

Lightbody Publishing, LLC

Copyright © 2021 by Yolanda Trevino

All rights reserved. No part of this book may be used or reproduced by any means, graphic, electronic, or mechanical, including photocopying, recording, taping or by any information storage retrieval system without the expressed written permission of the author except in the case of brief quotations embodied in critical articles and reviews.

The stories in this book reflect the author's recollection of events. Some names, locations, and identifying characteristics have been changed to protect the privacy of those depicted. Dialogue has been re-created from memory. Although the author has made every effort to ensure that the information in this book was correct at press time, the author does not assume and hereby disclaims any liability to any party for any loss, damage, or disruption caused by errors or omissions, whether such errors or omissions result from negligence or any other cause.

First printing, 2021. Revised February 22, 2022.

Lightbody Publishing, LLC
P.O. Box 151
Lafayette, CA 94549
www.LightbodyPublishing.com

For those that feel broken, lost or without a voice – I stand before you as a beacon of light. I see you. You are light, you are love, you are resilient and you are not alone. **My story is dedicated to all of you.**

"There is something in the human spirit that will survive and prevail, there is a tiny and brilliant light burning in the heart of man that will not go out no matter how dark the world becomes."

–Leo Tolstoy

TABLE OF CONTENTS

Introduction xi
Chapter 1 – Seven Seconds.. 1
Chapter 2 – Grandpa's House 7
Chapter 3 – Starling Avenue.. 11
Chapter 4 – Welcome To The Neighborhood 17
Chapter 5 – Spoons... 19
Chapter 6 – Buckle.. 23
Chapter 7 – Grandma 29
Chapter 8 – High School... 35
Chapter 9 – He Loves Me, He Loves Me Not 39
Chapter 10 – The Coworker 51
Chapter 11 – New Job 55
Chapter 12 – The Roommate.. 59
Chapter 13 – The Shoe Box 65
Chapter 14 – Bullshit Radar 71
Chapter 15 – Return To Zantaz 77
Chapter 16 – You've Been Served 83
Chapter 17 – Sleeping With The Enemy 87
Chapter 18 – Alternate Reality 95
Chapter 19 – Coercion.. 99
Chapter 20 – The Tables Have Turned 107
Chapter 21 – The Mask 111
Chapter 22 – Goodbye Nark... 119
Chapter 23 – Dead End... 131
Chapter 24 – Awakening... 139
Conclusion 151

INTRODUCTION

After the assault I drove home in shock, *what am I going to do? What should I do? I don't know what to do.* No one is going to believe me. My life had taken a terrible turn years ago and I tried to correct the misdirection but I couldn't after I had been ensnared to take a fall alongside my boyfriend for his misdeeds when Autonomy, his former employer, was in the throes of a multi-billion dollar conspiracy and it was about to be thwarted. To divert attention from their plot I was embroiled in a lawsuit when the conglomerate accused me of charges I didn't commit and coerced me into silence. The complex web of lies and deceit that tangled me had many sections, surprising twists and revelations, but in the end my life had been left in ruins. Too late to reminisce on what I missed because the past is history and history is in the past; I can't change it now. I had an unjust guilty charge hanging over me like a dark cloud and felt like a social leper. Now that I had just been date raped, no one would believe me or even care, I thought.

After a willful suicide attempt from attempting to escape the suffering from the many tragedies of my life, I survived and went through a spiritual awakening. This experience opened up a well of knowledge as to how my life had gotten so far off track. I had endured sexual assault, sibling abuse and relationships that in one form or another were exploitative and toxic to me. When I embarked on my journey of healing and self-discovery I recognized there were several traumatic experiences in my life that contributed to a broken spirit and feelings of low self-worth. I'd buried the pain and never worked through the emotional healing of them. I take you through those moments in this book and I'll explain how I turned everything around using various tools and practices that I discovered to help me adjust lifelong behaviors to overhaul my life. This helped me unleash a torrent of limitless potential to help me rise above the ashes in a short period of time. There have been many wonderful moments in my life too but for the purposes of identifying how I had fallen apart, I share what went wrong that started in childhood. I share these vulnerable moments to offer inspiration and empower others that have not only experienced traumas but to all that need reassurance that the human spirit is resilient and so is the healing power of the heart.

1
SEVEN SECONDS

People take one look at me and think I have my life so well put together; that I couldn't possibly know what trauma or victimization could feel like. We do after all judge a book by its cover and I'm aware that it only takes 7 seconds to make a first impression. With my hair styled, makeup on and business casual dress, I can appear to effortlessly finesse my way around a networking room leading with my smile, making acquaintances, chatting and greeting several familiar faces and friends in business. In the first 7 seconds as I pass through the checkout at the grocery store, the cashier takes notice of how healthy I eat and makes mention of all of the organic foods I place on her belt. Standing in my gym clothes, she and I make idle chit chat and she asks about fitness and beauty tips as I pass through her lane each week. In the first 7 seconds of meeting a client my sincere smile and warm demeanor immediately greets them and sets the tone that instantly quells their anxiety that I pick up on as they enter my clinic. In moments, the impression I emanate in every area of my life today is one of self-assuredness and confidence, a woman that encompasses a balance of both femininity and strength and also conveys sincerity and authenticity.

It also takes just 7 seconds for a predator to look for signs of weakness and vulnerability in someone they have targeted as their next victim[1]. Every 73 seconds someone in America is sexually assaulted, with 1 in 4 women being raped at some point in their life time[2]. Imagine how I felt when I became one of those statistics just days before my birthday.

No one would suspect by the way I carry myself today that just 4 short years ago I was living a very different existence. Struggling with depression at that time, a lack of self-esteem and a broken spirit from a series of events, I was living an emotionally depleted existence and an inauthentic life. I had suffered a nervous breakdown just a few years prior and finding that very difficult to recover from, I was given a cocktail of prescriptions that not only numbed out all emotional pain but any and all emotions whatsoever. The pills completely hindered my ability to think clearly let alone make rational decisions and they were very addictive. I became someone that I didn't recognize both inside and out. I had major weight gain and many side effects from the prescriptions; I ate and craved nothing but junk, I drank excessively at times and smoked a pack or more of cigarettes every day. Emotionally weakened and with a fragile state of mind, I felt like my life was already over as I was fast approaching my 40th birthday with no prearranged plans to celebrate.

Feeling lonely, I decided to get online and make a connection to see if I couldn't find a date to celebrate with. I had previously met and dated someone for several years that I had met online and didn't think anything of it when meeting my date, Mike, that way. We hit it off and spoke by text and phone and he asked me out on a date that Friday evening which was just a few days away. I spent a couple of hours getting ready for my date and recall feeling that no matter how much I tried to look my very best, I didn't feel that I did. My eyes had lost their sparkle, I was losing my hair from stress-related alopecia and I was so overweight, I felt ugly. After connecting with Mike, he invited me to dinner and said that he wanted to take me out to celebrate my birthday. I was really impressed by him, he was a restaurateur that lived in a really nice area and he planned to have a limousine waiting to take us to dinner. Without a thought to or regard for my safety, I felt excited and set off to meet my date at his home. With the limo and chauffeur waiting in the roundabout driveway we immediately set off to dinner after I had arrived.

With easy conversation throughout dinner, I felt comfortable enough to stay for a nightcap at his place when he invited me to stay afterward during the drive back. Once there one thing led to another and I definitely knew we were heading to the bedroom, but I wasn't prepared for what happened once inside. We kissed and undressed each other and then suddenly, Mike attacked me. I was startled and when I started crying he became even more aggressive and began to strangle me with one hand gripping my throat while he pinched off my nostrils with the other so that I couldn't breathe. I was in a panic and in the flash of a moment he pushed me back and wedged me between the bedroom wall and his dresser and forced me to the ground. He twisted my nose so hard, I felt a fiery sensation radiate across my entire face and I yelled out in pain while I tried to pull away but I couldn't move. It felt like he was breaking my nose and my face was very wet, I was suffocating and I thought I was bleeding. Everything was happening very quickly and when he released his grip on me I inhaled sharply and gasped for air and he forced himself into my mouth. On reflex, I began gagging and vomited on him and onto the carpet from both my mouth and nose. The wet sensation on my face was coming from my eyes. I was crying, naked and doubled over on my hands and knees, vomiting while struggling to breathe. Just as quickly as the attack had caught me off guard, he began dragging me by my hair onto the bed. The clips of my hair extensions were ripping out my hair and I knew there was no getting out of what was happening. I didn't have the physical strength to fight back and Mike pinned me down on the bed and positioned me in such a way that there was no escaping his lock on me and he raped me. I repeatedly cried out for him to stop and told him that he was hurting me but it only made things worse. The rape felt like it would never end and seemed to last an eternity. While being brutalized and held down, I stopped crying and escaped inward because I couldn't physically run away. I didn't want him to see that he put fear in me but it was too late.

When it was over he very casually rolled off of me and lay on the bed, out of breath. I felt as if I was witnessing what had happened in slow motion from outside of myself and I calmly and swiftly stood up, as if on autopilot. I put on my clothes and hurriedly gathered the remainder of my things. With my high heels in hand I walked very quickly to the front door and as I was reaching for the door lock, my arm felt like a heavy piece of rubber and looked as though it wasn't attached to body. I was trembling uncontrollably and it felt as though I was looking at myself from the outside. My hand was moving but it looked like someone else's hand that couldn't seem to turn the lock on the door. There was a fleeting thought that I might not get outside and my mind flashed to thinking of my Mom. In that moment I was five years old again and I wanted nothing more than to feel the safety that was wrapped in her embrace. I unlocked the door and briefly paused to slip on my shoes before getting outside. I wasn't thinking very clearly but my thoughts drifted to not wanting my feet to get cold or dirty. It was a very cold winter's night and as I opened the front door and hurried to my car the crispness of the air smacked me in the face. I was free and the air felt like life as it entered my lungs. I could hear the distant sound of Mike's voice from behind me but couldn't make out what he was saying, I didn't want to turn back to look or slow my pace. I got in the car, shut and locked the door and as he approached the driver side window, I was in reverse and then drove off as fast as I could.

I instantly felt to blame for what had happened to me and I just wanted to forget and wish it away, so I did not tell anyone. A time had come to pass where others had used me as a scapegoat for their ill-gotten gains and had taken advantage of me in ways I hadn't been capable of stopping and it severely and negatively impacted my life for many years if not forever. I had long ago lost my voice and the capability of defending myself. So many thoughts flooded into my mind but mostly I felt so worthless. Date raped and humiliated into silence. *This is what has become of me? Unable to defend myself, let alone speak up and tell anyone what has happened? How did my life get here? I don't even recognize myself anymore...*

2

GRANDPA'S HOUSE

When I was five we lived in a small rented house for a little over a year on Starling Avenue, which was a half mile from my paternal grandparents' house. I loved the time I spent with my Grandparent's and it was at this age that I have the most memories of happy times that I spent with them at their home. While Grandpa was at work there was no end to the fun things that my Grandmother and I did. I'd help her make fresh tortillas some days and on others, she would let me play in her dresses and heels that she kept tucked away in her bedroom closet. She made beautiful clothes and some of her dresses were handmade and others still hung with tags on them but she didn't go many places and never wore most of them. On other visits, she would set my hair and paint my fingernails while we sat on her bed waiting on my hair and nails to dry. We would watch old Hollywood movies or black and white TV show reruns while drinking Pepsi and eating chocolates. On warm sunny days, I would help her plant flowers in her garden patch in the back yard. While back there she would always warn me to stay away from the giant prickly pear that grew red fruit. The cactus was situated near the back fence line and one day my curiosity got the better of me; the glochids looked like her sewing needles but were white and as

I reached out to touch them they detached and buried themselves in my fingers.

"No lo toques mi hija, te va a pinchar" (Don't touch it my dear, it will poke you) she'd say when she'd catch me near it. Grandma had her back to me as she began to work the soil, her little flower patch was always being taken over by the dandelions. I started screaming and she rushed over. I was frantic and more scared than hurt but I was screaming and shaking my hands but they wouldn't fall out. She searched for her glasses that she had tucked in the front pocket of her apron. "Ay! Por que lloras?! Que pasa con eso? '" (Oh, why are you crying?! What's wrong, what is that?), she asked as I held my hands up for her to get a better look. "Oh, porbrecita, estas bien?" (Oh, poor baby are you ok?) She asked as she drew closer. "Get them out, get them out, Grandma!" I cried. "No te muevas, volveré enseguida, mi hija!" (Don't move; I'll be right back, little one!) And she rushed away and disappeared into the house. When she came back outside she had tissues and tweezers in hand and went right to work, quickly pulling each spike out as fast as she could. "Te amo mi chiquita, estás bien. Por favor, no toques eso otra vez. Voy a entra para hacerte un poco de leche tibia; entra" (I love you my little one, you're ok. Please, don't touch that again. I'm going inside to make you some warm milk; come inside) she said. Grandma was always so gentle and she never scolded me. Her touch always soothed and calmed me and as my cry reduced to a sniffle, she peppered the top of my head and my face with kisses and it made everything better. I shook my head from side to side and wiped away my tears with the back of my hands and I pointed to the rocking bench on the patio to let her know I was going to lay down outside. Warm milk always put me to sleep and when she went inside to prepare it, I pushed on the swinging bench before climbing on. As it rocked me, I lay on my back and stared into the sky looking for shapes in the clouds set against the blue sky. I could hear the distant humming sound of the small airplane that was circling to land at the nearby airport. Before she came back with my warm milk I had fallen fast asleep.

Later that afternoon Grandpa arrived home, I could always hear the sound of his truck parking out front when he came home from work. When I heard his keys unlocking the front door, I jumped from the couch and raced up to him as he walked in. Once inside he set down his thermos and lunchbox on the entry way tiles and got on one knee. He swept me up into a bear hug as I jumped into his arms and he rocked me side to side. "Grandpa, look! Look at what happened to me!" I said while holding up both hands for him to inspect. He titled his head back to adjust his sight and I watched his face intently to capture his reaction. "Oh! Lemme see that! Mi hijta, whaa happen to you?" he asked. He looked closely with his glasses to see the dots left behind from where the spikes had pricked me. "Grandpa, I got hurt." Before he could respond I continued, "But I'm ok now. Grandma fixed it and I fell asleep waiting for you! I'm so glad you're home, I missed you!" He always greeted me in the same way when he came into the house and Grandma filled him in on all of the details. He kissed my cheek after looking at my hands and he said, "Oh, Mi hija, I'm glad you're ok my little apple cheeks". I was born a natural red head and as a baby I had very puffy cheeks and when I would get overheated or when I would cry and get angry my face and cheeks would get very red. Grandpa always referred to me with this term of endearment. I loved spending time with them, they always made me feel safe and treasured and showered me with a lot of love and attention.

3
STARLING AVENUE

When we lived on Starling Avenue in the early 80's, there were many kids in the neighborhood. It was common to play outside until the street lamps came on, or whenever it was that you heard someone's Mom yelling from up the block to get home for dinner. Mom was pregnant and had my little sister while we lived there and Dad had broken his leg which kept him home and out of work for several months. My parents were very young when they started their family; Mom had my brother just a month before she was sixteen and I was born three years later. Mom worked and when she came home, she kept an immaculately clean house, made sure that we always had clean clothes to wear and prepared dinner every night. Dad always worked but he was home recovering from his broken leg and he spent a lot of time bonding and taking care of my sister while Mom was at work. When she was home he spent most of his time with his friends. Dad and I didn't spend much time together, he was emotionally closed off and I viewed him as the disciplinarian in our house. I was scared of Dad and was much more attached to Mom. I did my best to stay out of trouble but often times when my brother had gotten into mischief, he would point the finger at me to avoid getting punished and we'd both be spanked with a leather belt. When my world turned upside down while living on Starling Avenue, I couldn't find the courage to speak up about what was happening to me and had a very difficult time going to Dad for comfort and protection.

Jeffrey was the teenage boy that lived next door and he was having sex with the ten year old girl that lived across the street. To the left of her home lived my friend whom I frequently visited and there were bushes that separated their houses. One day as I left from play time, there were familiar voices that called out my name. As I approached the bushes Jeffrey pushed them open, exposing a hollow space from inside where he sat with the young girl on his lap. I could see she was wearing a dress and didn't have her underwear on. He reached for me and said, "Come closer". I was scared and shook my head from side to side while backing away and ran home. On another day as I was leaving from playtime, they both called out to me. "No, I'm not going over there!" I yelled out. "We aren't going to hurt you," I could hear Soriah say while she giggled. "Yeah we're not going to hurt you, come on, come here," Jeffery said. As I nervously approached the bushes, they opened quickly as I got near and I was grabbed by my arms as Jeffrey tried to pull me into the hollow space. "Help, help! Let me go!" They laughed at me and Jeffrey forced my hands to touch their genitals and before I could break free he thrust his hands in the front and back of my pants and put his fingers inside of me. I screamed out in terror and in pain as they continued to laugh. "You're such a baby," Soriah said. "You know you want it," Jeffery sneered as I cried. I was so afraid but I managed to break away and ran home. Once inside, I went straight into my room and didn't say anything about what he'd done and cried on my bed. I felt afraid to tell either of my parents but mostly, I was incapable of understanding or expressing what had happened. I was in physical pain and felt like I'd been scratched 'down there' but I otherwise didn't know what to call it. I felt uncomfortable and as though I had done something terribly wrong and I didn't want to get into trouble and be spanked for it so I kept silent.

Some time had passed and it was the summertime and I was playing in the front sprinklers and wandered over to our next-door neighbor's house. This really nice elderly woman with short brown hair and thick glasses lived there and anytime I would stop over to say hello she would offer me a chocolate mint; but I had forgotten she moved away when I rang the door-bell. I was expecting to see her smiling face open the door but instead it was a strange woman that I didn't recognize and when she invited me inside, I went in thinking I would see the woman with the brown hair and glasses. Instead, I saw this younger child who I frequently saw outside without his diaper; he hadn't learned to speak yet. These were new neighbors but I didn't know Jeffrey lived there and that standing before me was his Mom and sibling. She thought I was there to play and she pointed and told me to go to one of the back rooms and I did, I was still half expecting to see the brunette with the glasses. As I opened the door to the bedroom I was shoved from behind and fell to the ground on my face and started crying. I heard the bedroom door close behind me and I was rolled onto my back and saw that it was Jeffrey and his friend Patrick. I was still wearing my swimsuit from playing in the sprinklers and Jeffrey tore it off while Patrick clasped his hand down on my mouth and held my arms above my head with my wrists pinned together. Jeffrey detailed what he was going to do and he began poking and twisting at my nipples as he sat on my legs and I could see Patrick's braces above my face while they laughed. "I'm going first," Jeffrey said as they nodded to each other. I couldn't see; my tears were distorting my vision. Nobody could hear my muffled screams because

Patrick's hand was closed tightly over my mouth and in part covering my nose. I couldn't even move my head; I was panicking and couldn't breathe. I could hear knocking at the bedroom door and the strange woman was saying something but I couldn't understand her. The boys ignored the knocking but the knocking wouldn't stop, it got louder and the strange woman was trying to open the door. I couldn't understand what she was saying but suddenly the boys stopped and let me go. Jeffrey pulled up his pants and opened the door as I lay there naked and crying. She came in slowly and looked at them both and then looked at me on the floor and told me to get my clothes on and to go home. She didn't help me up or ask if I was ok and I thought by her tone that I had done something wrong. I was still crying and I got up in a hurry and put on my swimsuit bottoms and I ran to the front door while I clutched my top to my chest. I was trying to tie my swim top on but I was still learning to tie my shoes and I couldn't get it on without help. I waited at the front door and leaned into it like I wanted it to hug me and kept crying, I wanted to go home. I waited for the strange woman to appear so that she could help me tie my top on and I went back home, next door.

I wiped my tears away before I went inside, I felt sick but also uneasy because I wasn't sure of what would happen when I got in. I had a piercing and heavy fear in my chest and I wanted to throw up. I walked over to Mom as she sat in the recliner in our living room and Dad was sitting on the couch as they watched TV. I stared blankly at the screen unsure of what to say but Mom looked over at me and immediately could see that something was wrong. "What's the matter?" she asked gently. I was frozen in fear and I couldn't speak. "Babe, she can't talk! Something's wrong, something's happened!" she said and I could see that she looked worried. I kept trying to speak but I couldn't find my voice, I was mute. Mom became hysterical and Dad told her to calm down. As he looked at me he shook his head upward and furrowed his brows and said, "What's wrong? What's the matter with you?" I burst into tears and pointed downward and my Mom hugged me and said, "Tell me what happened, what's wrong? I need you to speak, use your words, I need you to tell me." "He hurt me!" I blurted out while I leaned into the safety of her embrace. "He pushed me down and his friend!" I was trying my best to explain but I didn't know how because I didn't understand what had happened. I was crying so hard and my words were a jumbled mess but they understood enough. "Who? Who did this to you?" they asked. I pointed next door and said, "He did it. That boy did it." My Dad flew out of the house in a rage and Mom reached for his shirt but he tore out of her grasp and she ran after him. I could hear a commotion and yelling outside and I ran to my room and hid in the closet in fear. When they came back in I came out and slowly peeked around the corner of the wall and I could see my Dad's face; he looked purple. My Mom came over to hug me and took me into the bathroom where she gave me a bath and put on my nightgown. I saw my grandparents the next day and as my Dad explained some of what had happened I could see the grief and sadness come over Grandma and Grandpa's face. Grandpa stayed quiet for a moment but he thought it was best to leave it alone. As a family we didn't speak of it again and my parents didn't call the police. We are of Native American/Spanish descent and my paternal grandparents migrated from Texas to California; Texas has had a long standing and unacknowledged struggle for equity of the Indigenous and Mexican peoples for more than one hundred years[3]. Fears are past down the lineage into the generations that follow and keep people within a culture suppressed from speaking out against further injustices for fear of retaliation, discrimination, humiliation, harm, etc. In the early 1980's racism was very prevalent in many towns across all states including here in California where they had migrated to and the decision to ignore what had happened to me was made so the family could move on. I was young and they'd thought I'd just forget it happened. However, trauma stays with you no matter how young you are when you experience it and with being assaulted as child and it being disregarded, I felt like it didn't matter and that I wasn't safe. This contributed to how I reacted to future traumatic experiences and before we moved from Starling Avenue, my brother started inappropriately touching me at bedtime. This went on intermittently over a three year period and I didn't know what to say or how to handle it and I kept silent about it for many years.

4

WELCOME TO THE NEIGHBORHOOD

We moved away from Starling Avenue soon after when my parents bought a home across town. I made many new friendships when we moved to our new neighborhood but there were some of our neighbors that didn't seem to be very welcoming. I began a friendship with two siblings that lived up the street soon after moving into our home and not long afterward their parents had asked me if the landscaping truck that was always parked outside of our house belonged to my dad. I told them that it did and a few days later I went back to play with the kids and they told me their dad said they couldn't play with me anymore. I asked why and could hear their dad tell them to shut the door but they just continued looking at me with blank stares. Their father came up from behind them and yelled at them for not listening to him and they scurried off as he slammed the door in my face. I cried on my walk home, I didn't understand why they suddenly didn't like me. We went to school together and continued to live up the street from one another for many years but we never spoke to each other again after that day. There was another neighbor, a man and his wife that lived two doors down from us. Anytime we would drive by the man would always scowl and make mean faces at us. It happened every time mom and I drove by and I knew it was intentional. I didn't understand why he was doing it; I had never spoken with him and didn't know who he was. He frightened me and when I played with other kids in the neighborhood that lived past his house, I would walk around the block to avoid walking past his home if I were alone. One Saturday my friend and I were walking back from her house to mine and we were just nearing my neighbor's house. I could see that he came outside with an angry look on his face and he grabbed at his keys from his pants pocket and walked quickly to his car. I was slowing riding my bike while my friend walked on my right side; I was afraid of him and kept my face turned towards her and continued talking. She stopped walking and a look of surprise came over her face when suddenly my neighbor ran into me with his car. He got out of his car and yelled, "You stupid kid, next time watch where you're going goddamn it! You won't be so lucky if it happens again! Do you understand me? Get out of here!" He pulled at my arm until he had me on my feet. He wrenched my bike out from under his bumper and shoved it at me. I wasn't terribly hurt but more shaken and my new bike had a few scratches but my friend and I hurried off. My dad wasn't home and I didn't say anything to mom about what had happened. I never looked in his direction again when we drove by and fortunately they moved not long after we moved in. I was barely six years old and I didn't understand what racism was before these incidents but I recognized we were being treated differently and that it had to do with the color of our skin and our Hispanic ethnicity. Some of the neighbors treated our family like we didn't belong there but most were very welcoming. Mom and dad worked hard and owned their home alongside everyone else and dad took pride in making the front yard look so beautiful that it stood out as the best property on the block.

5
SPOONS

I made many new friends when I started my new school. I had also taken a liking to reading and school was very easy for me. I'd have everything done and would often be asked to start on my homework or read a book while the other students were still doing their daily lessons to keep me from being a social butterfly and interrupting the others.

Throughout elementary many of my friendships were with kids that had some form of chaos and abuse going on in their home. As a child, I didn't recognize that on a subconscious level we tend to gravitate towards those that have similar experiences. Soon after we moved to our new home my brother's behavior changed and he became very aggressive and had outbursts that frightened me. I was different than most children in some way, I had nurturing quality and most all of my friends confided in me at a young age and as I got older would look to me for advice.

My brother Adam is older than me by three years. Before his behavior changed I remember that he was a sensitive and shy kid and he was bullied by one of his teachers when we started our new school. His teacher singled him out because he couldn't see well and also had a nervous tick in his eyes. She'd ridiculed him in front of the other students and it had escalated into her constantly hitting him on his head with her ring. I tagged along with mom when she went to our school and put a stop to it by giving the teacher a piece of her mind. Mom told the teacher in no uncertain terms that she'd use her ring on her head if she had to come back. The teacher left him alone after that.

Adam and I had different interests and separate friends and he was always getting into mischief like boys do but it would cause him to be disciplined. Dad used to spank us both if Adam had done something wrong but over time dad stopped spanking me for things I didn't do and Adam felt it was unfair. We both had difficulty talking with dad about anything that upset us because we feared him and acting out gave my brother attention if even it was to get punished. His angry tantrums were a constant and eventually grew into violence, psychological and physical abuse towards me and later it was directed at my parents too. This started when I was six and went on until I was sixteen. Anything at all could set his mood off from one direction and into another. His behavior was very extreme and started to become dangerous when he maimed our family pet when I was nine after one of his usual violent outbursts. On this particular day after school, he was eating peanut butter from a spoon and suddenly grew very angry and he threw his spoon across the room. I was sitting at the dining table doing homework when he started shouting and started taking spoons from the drawer and throwing them in my direction. This aggression was very typical and normal behavior for him now. I was ducking out of the way and put my head on the table when he ran up to me and came to an abrupt halt, I thought he was going to hit me so I covered my face but instead he reached down and grabbed our cat. Pokey was lying near my feet basking in a sun spot that was filtering in from the sliding glass door.

Adam opened the glass door to the patio and threw Pokey against the wall and he fell and tried to run off but Adam picked him up and started bashing his head into the concrete over and again. I screamed out and begged Adam to stop but he wouldn't and I could hear Pokey cry out but mostly he was only making guttural sounds. When Adam had exhausted himself he threw the cat down like he was discarding a stuffed animal and he walked off to his room. Pokey couldn't move and had blood and liquid oozing out of his ears, nose and mouth. His eyes had rolled into the back of his head and they were moving in different directions. I cried and held him as he lay limply in my arms and brought him into the house. I didn't know what to do and mom was due to come in soon so I placed Pokey on the couch and went to my room and locked the door. I was afraid of Adam. She didn't notice him until later in the evening and I could hear the worry in her voice when she asked what had happened to the cat, but Adam quickly spoke up and said he'd noticed that Pokey looked like he'd been in a fight and gave me a smirk. I didn't say anything and cried myself to sleep that night. Pokey was in such bad shape but after that night we didn't see him again, he had run off.

6

BUCKLE

Around this time I started talking more with my parents about what was going on at home but dad didn't seem to think it was unusual. He mostly wasn't there to witness Adam's behavior but he could see that many things in our home were being broken and went missing. When he'd ask us kids about it, I would tell him but nothing changed. Years had went by with Adam having very aggressive and violent outbursts but he mostly kept his behavior hidden when mom and dad was home. In the first decade of my adolescent years, Dad would be gone all week working and leave early in the mornings on the weekends to hang out with his friends. Although Mom also worked she kept the house, did the laundry, cooked, shopped and reared us for the most part and dad was the disciplinarian. Mom rarely saw her friends and was home all of time taking care of us. This imbalance in their relationship took an emotional toll on mom many times and she'd take her anger out on us by shouting and yelling at us quite a bit during these years. We didn't visit mom's family and I didn't have maternal grandparents, they had died when mom was very young. Mom experienced many of her own traumas at a young age and her life turned upside down when she was orphaned and the family members that were entrusted to care for her and her siblings were horribly abusive. Although she and her siblings were split amongst family, they stayed in touch over the years but the abuse and trauma that they endured as kids haunted them into their adult life and some of them past away early in life. We didn't form strong bonds with most of her relatives. Mom didn't have help or anyone to turn to for advice or guidance when it came to relationships or raising us and when my parents were having problems they separated for a very short time. Mom had left for only a few weeks but it felt like years. It happened that she left one evening after they argued in their room; mom and dad didn't argue very much in front of us so when she had suddenly left I was shocked and scared. I felt so abandoned; I didn't know if she was coming back. The house had a very heavy presence when she was gone and I was so anxious that I couldn't sleep and I was suffering from night terrors and waking up drenched in sweat. Dad was sad and withdrawn but he and I didn't usually talk about much so it didn't feel different between us other than he was home now and mom was gone. I was ten years old and Easter was a week away but we weren't feeling very excited about celebrating so we didn't have any plans made and didn't talk about it. It was Saturday and I woke up early with my sister; Adam had spent the night at a friends and Dad was going to take us to breakfast so Gwen and I got into the shower together to get ready in a hurry. We started arguing about who was going to wash their hair first and I didn't want to hear the scolding that was sure to follow after our shower, so I let her use the shampoo and she got soap in her eyes. She started screaming and I was sure to be blamed and was worried about it so I quickly tried to calm her down and rinse out her eyes. When we finished showering we opened the glass shower door to grab our towels and dad stormed in with his leather belt and the large metal buckle was still attached. He started beating us without discretion on where he hit or how he swung his belt. I got whipped three times and once in the face before I ran out of the bathroom screaming but my sister was left behind and was cornered. She bore the brunt of his beating and she shrieked in terror and in pain. I ran back to help her and could see she was crouched down holding her towel like a teddy bear but I ran away again. She was screaming and as each whip reigned down upon her she screamed louder and there was nothing I could do. I was familiar with spankings when we got into trouble but he had never hit her before and now he was beating her with the belt. I didn't know what to do. He kept hitting her with such force and far more than he had ever hit Adam or me, it sounded like it would never end. I was so scared of what he was doing and that he was going to come back to finish with me too so I locked my door and paced in a circle, I was so terrified that I peed a little on the carpet. I heard him stop but Gwen continued screaming. I waited to hear him leave the bathroom and I opened my door and quietly ran to her. When I entered the bathroom she was still crouched down and she was shaking uncontrollably and cried out to me for help by shrieking louder when she saw me; I grabbed her hand and we ran back to our room and locked the door behind us. I held her in my arms as we cried. I just wanted mom. *This house has gone crazy! What am I going to do? I just want mom. Where's mom?! This would never have happened if she was here; I hate dad! I hate him! I hate mom for leaving me here!* My sister had bruises and welts all over her body and she also had a swollen face and bruising on her eye. Dad had completely lost all control. The mood was very somber for the day and later that afternoon, we came out of our room and ignored him as we came into the kitchen so that I could prepare us something to eat. He was sitting near the kitchen and we walked by him but he held his arms out to us and we ran to him and together we all started crying. He apologized for what he'd done and dad never hit my sister and me again. Mom came back to visit with us the following weekend and had bought us each an Easter basket and an outfit but she didn't notice the faded bruises on my sister. I felt this tight feeling in my chest and in my throat like I wanted to cry and tell her everything but I didn't, we missed her so much and I didn't want to spoil the moment. We didn't say anything about what had happened.

Mom came home a few weeks later and things went back to our dysfunctional normal. Dad wasn't home and Mom got started with cleaning. I was helping her and Gwen was told to go to her room because she was in the way of mom trying to vacuum. We were caught by surprise when Adam charged out of his bedroom and ran into the living room. He jumped on the back of the couch and hovered over us with clenched fists and shouted like a maniac for her to stop hitting Gwen. Mom told him to stop shouting and to go to his room but when he jumped off of the couch he put her in a head lock and wrestled her to the ground. I grabbed Gwen to try to shield her from looking on as we screamed in fright for him to let her go. He wrenched harder on his choke hold and mom could hardly talk but was yelling for him to get off of her but he overpowered her. She continued kicking but he kept choking her until she went limp and he wrenched on her neck even tighter before he released her. She immediately gasped for air and laid there trying to catch her breath. My sister and I ran to her and I screamed for him to get out and he ran out of the house. He was always angry with mom and dad for many things but he was taking his anger out on her for dad having beaten Gwen while they were separated, however mom never knew it happened. When dad came home that night, he could no longer be in denial about the seriousness of Adam's behavior. He had given mom whiplash and she continued to go to work and provide for us while she recovered. Dad started working nights so that he could be home during the day time and things subsided for a while. Whenever our parents weren't around, Adam continued his aggressive behavior and would isolate Gwen and say false things about me and my parents that I would overhear. He is nine years older than Gwen and he did this often to manipulate the facts in an effort to control her impressionable mind so that she continued to look up to him and excuse his violence that she'd witness. Aside from the beating my dad had given Gwen, he had not hit her again and continued to spoil her with his affection and attention and she was treated very fondly. Adam and I weren't given that same level of attention in our first decade of life and Adam and I both resented it but he would tell Gwen terrible things in an attempt to get someone on his side. This distorted her reality from how she knew us to be.

I was living with overwhelming anxiety and feelings of fear and self-loathing that I began to have an irrational fixation with my weight as a means for control in my life. I was a good kid that didn't test boundaries, I didn't act out or cause many problems and I was easy to parent. I wasn't without my faults but Mom and dad didn't have to worry about me and could focus their attention mostly on my siblings. I pretended as though I was fine by staying out of the way and keeping busy but I held everything inside. Grandma was ill and I didn't see my grandparents much anymore. I spent a lot of time with friends but when I was home, I usually kept to myself with reading and maintained a sharp focus on school work. I was a scholastic over-achiever and had skipped a grade shortly after starting middle school and I tried to be as perfect as possible so as not make waves or cause disappointment. The differences in our personalities, behavior and the type of attention we were given by our parents caused resentment between us siblings over time; but I had developed my own unhealthy coping mechanisms just as they had. I was emotionally surviving with maladaptive behaviors such as perfectionism, people pleasing, controlling behaviors and an unhealthy body image. By comparison to my extremely thin siblings, I looked bigger and I became hyperaware of every nuance and change in my body as I was developing. I learned how to count calories, frequently weighed myself and I began dieting and restricting my food in the first decade of my life. Any time I was feeling emotionally lost these behaviors became a cycle of coping that created a love/hate relationship within myself that lasted throughout most of my life.

7

GRANDMA

I wasn't close with my grandparents anymore and I didn't have them to turn to for guidance or advice. A couple of years after we moved from Starling Avenue, Grandma started showing signs of depression and unfortunately my regular visits and time spent there was short lived. There was still so much to be learned about mental health and my grandparents grew up during the WW2 era; the ignorance at that time surrounding depression meant that you were deemed insane and sent away to live out your life in an asylum. In the 1980's her diagnosis was still completely misunderstood and stigmatized and grandpa was concerned that others would find out and worried over what they might think.

When she "fell ill" and before she began her medication, I was asked to look after her and I missed two weeks of school to stay with her while my Grandfather went to work. I kept busy with crafts and when she wasn't napping she looked after me and was the same gentle, loving Grandma I knew her to be. Although she slept a bit more than usual and she see seemed sad to me, she and I spent time together like most other days. "Estas bien, Grandma?" (Are you ok, Grandma?) I asked her. "Mi hija, estoy bien. No escuches nada de lo que digan, solo estoy cansado. Nunca me escucha. El abuelo no me escucha y estoy cansado de eso." (My little one, I'm ok. Don't listen to anything they say, I'm just tired. He never listens to me. Grandpa doesn't listen to me and I'm tired of it), she said. As tears sprang to her eyes, she waved her hand in the air in frustration and for me not to pay any mind as she shook her head. I believed her. At times their arguing would get so loud that I would place my hands over my ears and do my best to tune them out while watching television and scream out to them, "Callate! I'm trying to watch TV!" I didn't see this manner of speaking as abnormal. They were very loving and doted on me, but their yelling at each other was common to hear and their loud arguing happened every time I was there for as far back as I could remember. Grandma could always be heard saying, "Escuches me! Escuches me!" (Listen to me! Listen to me!) while trying to gain understanding from Grandpa but he'd often reply, "Eh, Callate la boca! Estas loca, callate. No quiero escucharte hablar mas!" (Hey, shut your mouth! You're crazy, shut up. I don't want to hear you talk anymore). While I had taken an early winter break from school to watch over her, no one asked me how we interacted. They didn't inquire as to whether she behaved like herself or what our days were like together. During this time, it was clear to me that she was frustrated with my Grandfather and when he would come home, she would go back into her room and lay down. He assumed she'd spent all of her time asleep while I was there and didn't ask me otherwise. At the time, I was too young to understand the dynamics of what was going on and our visits abruptly stopped. I missed her beyond words but I was expected to quietly accept it and not ask questions.

She relied strictly on my Grandfather to speak on her behalf when she needed medical care. No one took into consideration that grandma was experiencing emotional exhaustion or that she was could be experiencing a delayed trauma response to things from her past. I learned as I grew older there were many terrible injustices that my gentle grandmother had been subjected to before she'd met grandpa. I also knew by the way she and grandpa spoke to each other that she suffered from relationship woes and was saddened from being mistreated for so long. She had reached a breaking point in their arguing – I'd seen the same cycle play out amongst my parents and other relationships within the family as well. As I grew older, I recognized the men in my family were misogynistic and they did as they pleased. Speaking out against mistreatment was deemed out of line, inappropriate and disrespectful. Financially the women in my family typically didn't make enough money to support themselves and couldn't afford to take a break from the chaos of life for very long. They were still expected to be homemakers, have kids and rear them.

Grandpa didn't comprehend the medical issues or terminology to properly express to medical professionals as to what she was experiencing and her mental health was mishandled. He felt it was best to keep everyone from coming to see her and rather than he and their sons being more supportive of her, she was neglected and isolated in her home. When she started taking medication no one understood what she was experiencing and instead mistook her for getting worse and going crazy when she became delusional as a side-effect to her medication. None of us understood this at the time that she was having side-effects. Elderly people are more prone to psychosis as a side-effect to many types of prescriptions and any age group can experience the same if given the wrong medication from a misdiagnosis. Her depression diagnoses then changed to paranoid Schizophrenic and she was kept on these pills for many years. At times her behavior would change for the worse and no one understood that it was because of a new prescription or dosage change. There were instances when the medication was too expensive and they couldn't afford it and she'd go for long periods of time when she didn't take them; she suffered through painful withdrawals and would become agitated and angry as a result. After a long while, grandma's talkative demeanor would come back and you could see the clarity in her eyes. I didn't understand any of this myself at the time but through a similar experience of my own with prescription medication many years later, I know in my heart this is what she experienced.

After the age of eight, I rarely visited her anymore but throughout the years when I did, I could see that she was clear thinking when she wasn't on the medications and had someone to talk to. All of the men in her life disregarded her presence as though she were invisible. Grandma didn't drive or have friends, she wasn't from California and she didn't speak English in the predominantly white neighborhood that she lived in and when she needed to see specialists, the Doctors in town didn't speak Spanish. She was surrounded by family and was very lonely.

I was in my mid-twenties when grandpa died. In the few years before he passed away he shared many stories of regret for his choices and behavior in life and he acknowledged that he didn't know how to properly care for her mental health. When he died unexpectedly, Grandma was left in the care of their eldest son who had stayed living with them most of his life. She passed away a few years after grandpa died. She was admitted to the hospital because she wasn't eating, and we were horrified to see that she was emaciated and had bruises on her body and bed sores. She was discharged from the hospital into the care of my parents but had contracted pneumonia and passed away within a few weeks. Her life had been upended and she was met with a devastating end that broke my heart. I miss them both and think of them often and when I pray for guidance I can feel that her gentle spirit is with me.

8
HIGH SCHOOL

I started a new school and I was excited but very quickly the novelty of new beginnings and meeting new people wore off. Adam started spreading hurtful rumors that tarnished my reputation and instigated arguments between me and other kids. One day before school he had beaten me in front of his girlfriend to intimidate her after one of their arguments enraged him. Several weeks later he was in a fit of anger and screaming at me and ran to grab his hunting knife. He came to me and withdrew the dagger from the holster as if to stab me but he ran off and instead stabbed and sliced through the wood on his dresser. I wasn't safe at home and I became very withdrawn and angry. I was reacting to the abuse by becoming defensive towards everyone. I started getting into fights at school, suspended, skipping classes, drinking and smoking marijuana to escape and my grades plummeted to barely passing. I was the academic that mom and dad didn't have to worry about but I had suddenly shifted and lost interest in things that mattered to me. I no longer read, played sports or took up music lessons. Two teachers could see something was wrong and had spoken with me privately and knew I was going through a crisis. I was grateful they each worked out a plan with me to pass my classes because I otherwise wouldn't have. Mom and dad were at their end with how to handle Adam's behavior and he had started hitting dad during arguments. I was now giving them additional grief but I was largely misunderstood about why. I didn't know until years later that they had looked into having Adam removed from the home and sent to a reform school - a boot camp for troubled teens. Camp personnel described how they would take him from his room while he was sleeping so that he would put up less of a fight because the students didn't go willingly, but mom and dad were unsettled with that and decided against it. They recognized something was terribly wrong and they didn't want to cause him further distress but were heavy hearted in their decision because he was endangering all of us and they felt helpless because neither could stay home from working. As a family, we didn't speak about these horrific events and we didn't tell anyone outside of the home either, it was an unspoken family matter that we kept private. The abuse had been a constant in my life and was insufferable, I felt badly about it but it was our normal.

My parents announced we were moving out of town at the end of my school year and I wasn't excited about the move. I felt anxious and unhappy that I was going to be in a new town where I didn't know anybody and a change for the better seemed bleak and hopeless. No one asked for my input on how I felt about moving away; I wasn't close with my grandparents anymore and I was leaving all of my friends behind. Fuck this, I thought.

Our home life problems were paled in comparison to the news that broke out during the last week of school. As we headed into the summer of 1991, a classmate at Granada High had gone missing and the school was in frenzy when we learned that Jessica McHenry had been abducted and was found burning on the side of the back roads. All teens knew where Tesla Road was, everyone that learned to drive had at some point driven along that back road. It was a long and desolate country road on the outskirts of our town. I had known Jessica as a child, she lived across the street from our elementary school and we used to play together on occasion at her house. She was quiet, shy and very kind; and she always had a beautiful, big smile for everyone when she said hello. She beamed a beautiful ray of light and I was sick when I'd heard of her murder. Only two years before, another young teen, Ilene Misheloff, had been abducted. Ilene was a 13 year old girl that disappeared in 1989 while walking home from school in the neighboring town of Dublin, CA. It was a frightening reality to know that there was a child abductor on the loose and now there was a killer on the streets and everyone in school and in town was afraid as we headed into summer.

We moved to Tracy, CA into our new home and we spent the summer there. Adam continued his behavior very shortly after we started attending our new high school. It started out as a new beginning and I didn't have to worry about him spreading rumors because he didn't know anyone. He stayed wanting to hang out with me during all of the breaks between classes because he didn't make new friends there and he complained and was angry with my parents for moving us there. He was asked to leave after another of his violent outbursts after school that sent me running outside to get away from him. He was angry with his girlfriend that still lived in Livermore and they'd just had an argument and he hung up the phone after screaming at her. He was seething in anger and opened the fridge and grabbed a soda can and in a rage he threw it at my face and barely missed me as I quickly dodged it and it grazed my hair. I ran out of the house crying and sat down on the curb and waited for mom to come home. When dad arrived both of my parents asked him to leave, he was already eighteen now, but he stayed unapologetic and resentful towards us. He wouldn't acknowledge his abuse or take accountability for what he had done to me or to all of us throughout my childhood and teen years. I tried to have a friendship with him years later but I saw him infrequently. Over time his behavior hadn't changed, he was inappropriate the last time I visited with him and it made me uncomfortable and I decided that it's best to remain estranged.

9

HE LOVES ME, HE LOVES ME NOT

Aadi was my first love and one of my best friends in high school after I moved to Tracy, CA. He and I were crazy about each other yet the rumors of his infidelities had started very soon after we began our relationship. "Babe, hey, you know me. Don't let anything happen to us," he'd said while hugging me when I cried to him the first time I heard the gossip that pierced my heart. I felt like the wind had been knocked out of me when a friend of mine told me she'd seen him kissing someone else. We started dating after I graduated high school in the summer of 94' and had met in class during my sophomore year at Tracy High School. He knew what it felt like to be the new kid on the block, he'd arrived to America only two years before and we quickly became good friends when he introduced me around. When I first noticed him I heard him speaking Spanish and I had mistaken him for being Hispanic but he was from India. He had large brown expressive eyes, a beautiful olive complexion with golden flecks in his brown hair that glistened in the sunlight. I was fascinated and wanted to know more about him and his culture. Aadi and I saw each other in class and spoke regularly each day throughout our school day and were very close friends first, we had a love that started very naturally and was based on friendship. I felt he was trustworthy and that he was someone that I could confide in. When we became a couple I trusted him blindly and allowed myself to be very vulnerable, I believed him when he told me people didn't want to see us together and that it was just gossip.

We were from different cultures and it was difficult to navigate at first because our families were unsupportive. When he introduced me to his parents they disapproved from the moment they'd met me. His mother didn't attempt to hide her disdain the moment we were introduced and she sat me down and explained that she was preferred to arrange his marriage from a selection of more 'suitable' brides within his culture. I was so nervous and excited to meet them and I was heartbroken that his parents didn't accept me. I was seventeen and in love with him but deemed unworthy because of my ethnicity and culture. As she continued on I held it together for as long as I could and I burst into tears and yelled at her that she was being cruel to me before I left their home in a hurry and drove away. Her opinions remained strong throughout our relationship and continuously interfered and drove a wedge between us. Although my parents also weren't very accepting of our relationship at the beginning, I wasn't going to allow anyone to interfere in who I chose to love and they grew to accept it.

After we turned eighteen, he bought me a ring and we got engaged. Aadi and I talked about our future and we moved in together but we didn't make any immediate plans to get married and quickly settled into making a life together. He had a circle of friends from high school that he continued to stay close with and I didn't interfere in him wanting to have boys' night out but after we moved in together the rumors of infidelities started surfacing and it was starting to erode my confidences in our relationship. Two years into our relationship I was involved in two altercations with an ex-girlfriend from his high school days after she began harassing me. We'd gotten into a fight after I came out of the grocery store from shopping one evening when she tried to accost me. On another late evening while I was driving into town on my way home I was caught off guard when someone attempted to run me off the road. I didn't realize who it was until I caught up with her and saw her in the driver side window before she ran through the red light and sped off. She was clearly imbalanced and jealous but he denied having an affair with her and said they weren't in contact. I didn't trust he was telling me as truth and I left him. He begged for me to come back and said that I was letting someone else get between us that he'd long ago forgotten about and didn't care for. We were passionate and we often fought like two prideful lions but we would always make up with intense lovemaking. We frequently broke up and got back together over rumors and silly arguments and it became a vicious cycle of codependency and it felt like an addiction to each other; I wanted to believe that he was telling me the truth and I went back to him.

Our relationship was irrevocably changed during the fall of 1996. I was nineteen, Aadi and I had been together for two years. I was visiting my parents at their home one day when I became violently ill. I was doubled over afterward with an excruciating pain in my lower abdomen and I could hardly walk and began crawling. Dad rushed me to the hospital as fast as he could and blew through all of the stop signs and lights to get me there. After we arrived at the hospital dad went to get help and staff quickly carted me into a room and after they helped me onto a gurney bed I started bleeding and a doctor quickly arrived. After a series of hurried tests she said I was suffering from an ectopic pregnancy.

Mom was with me while I lay there in excruciating pain and the doctor explained what was happening and that I was hemorrhaging and that death was imminent if I didn't have emergency surgery. I was afraid and confused; I didn't know I had been pregnant. Suddenly I was facing death and making decisions about my fertility. I didn't know what to do but I didn't want to have the surgery, I didn't have money to pay this bill and I also was afraid to be put to sleep. I didn't know if I'd wake up. I started crying and was thinking irrationally from the shock of what was happening and mom and the doctor pleaded with me to sign the paperwork so that I could be taken into the ER. I finally said ok and they immediately carted my gurney off and rushed me into the operating room while I began scribbling my name on each page. I was terrified of what was happening. When we had first arrived I had dad page Aadi but he still hadn't shown up to the hospital. He was supposed to be at his parents' house and they lived practically across the street, just two minutes' drive away. *Where is he?!* I begged the doctor to let me wait just five more minutes for him to arrive but my life was in peril and she said she couldn't wait. I went into hysterics all of a sudden and mom started crying. "Mom, I'm scared that I won't wake up! Tell dad I love him and tell Aadi I love him too if I don't wake up! No, no, wait, doctor wait, please, please wait, stop, please…!" I implored as the anesthesiologist put me under.

When I woke from surgery he still hadn't come to the hospital or phoned back. I was so hurt. I hadn't known I was pregnant, I just faced near death and had emergency surgery and woke up to half of my fertility removed. I was devastated and overwhelmed with grief that I had been pregnant and it had gone terribly wrong and Aadi wasn't there for me. It seemed as though my life didn't matter to him and I felt so worthless and unloved. After I'd been discharged from the hospital, he didn't say more other than he was with friends that day even though he'd told me earlier that he was visiting his parents. I didn't want anyone to know what had happened and while I recovered I told people I had a cyst removed. I was dealing with a mix of many emotions and felt like no one understood what I was going through so I struggled with my grief alone. I became depressed and went on anti-depressants after seeing a psychiatrist. I was experiencing post-partum depression but no doctor had ever explained that to me or alerted me to the possibility of unexpected changes in behavior after my surgery. I also suffered from thyroid issues, severe depression and anxiety for over two decades at various times in life that started immediately after my ectopic surgery. The anti-depressants I was prescribed caused so much weight gain and mood swings, I didn't recognize that these changes were negative side-effects of the pills because I was already feeling low in energy and irritable before taking them and now my moods were far worse and swinging from one extreme to the other. It was difficult to navigate the uncontrollable and unexpected behavioral changes and anger that followed after the surgery and the ignorance of my health issues and his lack of support created a huge burden in our relationship.

Aadi and I stayed together for five more years but our relationship eroded. I had a huge emotional disconnect from him for not being there for me and it created bigger problems for us as I became withdrawn. He responded with becoming very possessive and controlling and I began wearing long sleeves and pants year round even as the summers went into the triple digits in an attempt to become invisible. I was emotionally depleted and began sleeping a lot and gaining more weight - I was suffering from an unrealized hormonal imbalance caused by the surgery which was exacerbated with ill side-effects from the medication I'd been prescribed. All of my friendships were affected and because Aadi didn't like any of them, it was difficult to see them or speak with them by phone. If I'd made plans to see anyone, we'd argue before I was set to leave and it would ruin my day or evening so that I wouldn't want to go anywhere. Afterward he didn't have to take responsibility for keeping me home because I had made the choice to stay. He had a different set of standards for himself and I was feeling very suppressed. My loathing turned our arguments into violence as my anger grew to rage which always left me feeling with magnified shame and guilt atop of what I was already living with day to day. I kept thinking I could improve myself and that if I stayed things would get better between us. It wasn't as though he hit me, Aadi wasn't like that. He'd slapped me once or twice and pulled my hair during some very heated arguments, but I had usually provoked it. Our quarrels would cease for about two days before the same arguments brought us back to fighting like crazy over the same issues and it went on like this for most of our relationship. I developed major anxiety and one evening my symptoms went into over drive and I thought I was having a heart attack and went to the hospital and was told I was experiencing a severe anxiety attack.

While Aadi continued a social life with his friends, my life consisted of working and staying home and I was doing everything on my own and stopped cooking and cleaning for the both of us. Over time our house became a place neither of us wanted to be and the long nights he spent with friends turned into coming home the following mornings. I knew he was being unfaithful. He denied it when I confronted him and said that I was crazy and that I had turned into a jealous and insecure person when I used to be so confident. I knew he was addicted to sex - our weekends together were spent watching porn, ordering take-out, smoking marijuana and drinking. We were in our early twenties now and no longer in high school, I couldn't live like that anymore. We were both so unhappy but I was the only one going to therapy, taking on all the blame and trying to salvage what we had but nothing changed.

In the last several months of our relationship he was flagrantly disrespectful and was seen by my parents driving around town in my new European car with another woman that wasn't his mother. Aadi stopped next to my parents at a stop light but he denied it when I confronted him. The same argument had gone on for months after I had found someone else's hair in my car and in my bed and someone had stepped on and broken my eye glasses that were in my home. I'd found chewing gum smeared all along the back of the passenger seat in my new car but he said I was nuts and that I liked to make up stories. I'd had enough of his lies and betrayal. I used to think we had life goals together and something to look forward to with a brighter future on the horizon, but I was the only that worked hard for that. Even while I was depressed I was working hard to get ahead in life. When I began making more money than him, he spited me for it. I could no longer see my future with him in it and decided to move out.

During our last month together there was an accident when Aadi's dog jumped the fence and nearly killed the neighbor's dog. They kept feeding him over the fence line but we'd repeatedly asked them not to because although he was friendly dog, he was also a large, strong and territorial Staffordshire terrier. Aadi wasn't around when the neighborhood swarmed around the dogs and screamed in terror while I had to break up a dog fight. He had been leaving several times each week – saying he needed to put gas in his car from the station that was a minute drive away. He'd be gone for two hours and then scream at me when I became upset. I'd called him several times to no avail and when he decided to make his way home, the police had called animal control and the dog was gone and being put down. My own safety had been compromised and given the excuses for his absence, I was incapable of shelving my feelings to console his grief and he detested me for it.

It was September 2001, we were moving out of our house at the end of the month – we had each found separate apartments and I was moving out of town. Life was chaotic for the world, everyone was frightened and thought the world was ending when 9/11 happened and yet he and I were separating. The stress from life was overwhelming for me and in a moment of weakness I wanted to stay together but he encouraged me to move along with my plans and said he was ready to move on too. I agreed and tried to keep things amicable; I had given him money for the security deposit and first month's rent on his apartment. Moving day arrived and we slept in a little and I laid there in his arms after we made love. We were always intimate throughout our relationship and it was rare that we weren't. As we lay there together we talked about the move and we agreed that we would meet up at his apartment so that I could pick up my vacuum that I was loaning to him. I showered and came back to the bedroom and saw he'd taken something important to me from my dresser drawer, I had seen it was there before the shower. When I questioned him about it he denied it and immediately got angry, saying to me that I was causing problems just as I always had. I was incensed from all of the lies, he just couldn't be honest about anything big or small and I began screaming at him to give my belongings back and went into the bathroom to calm down. When I was done drying my hair and came back out of the bathroom, I'd seen my belongings had been neatly placed back in my dresser and he gave no explanation about it whatsoever. The rest of our day together was left feeling spite and resentment towards one another. He'd asked if he could still continue to borrow my vacuum and I'd said yes and he took it with him. We agreed to meet the upcoming Sunday at his place for me to pick it up.

    I had given him all of my furniture, kitchenware, bought him toiletries and also given him money to get his place because he was floating between jobs. Even though we were parting ways I still tried to help him so he could get on his feet. The breakup was hard for me and I thought he felt the same way, we had spent eight years of our lives together and two of those years started out as best friends in high school. He was family and a huge part of my life; I wanted to have my vacuum back but mostly it seemed like reason enough to see each other. I also wanted to make sure he was doing ok and settled in. Ironically, he had moved into the same apartment unit that we had once shared many years ago as a new couple starting out with nothing. I wasn't sure what to think about it. We moved and the weekend was closing, I had called ahead before I left and he didn't answer so I drove the hour drive to Tracy and went to his place. I saw his car parked in the carport and I walked through the echoes of time along the familiar pathway that led to the door of our first apartment. It felt like déjà vu, the memories and familiarity of when we had started out together here flooded my mind and those moments felt like they'd happened only yesterday. It was a bittersweet walk to his door, not ours, but his now. I knocked and as I waited for him to answer I could hear him ask someone to check on who was at the door and I saw Daisy, the imbalanced and jealous ex-girlfriend, peer out from behind the vertical blinds in the dining room. Her eyes widened in surprise when she saw it was me. Behind her was all of my furniture in the same place we had kept things when he and I had lived there years ago - it felt as if everything was frozen in time. Life had come full circle and she and I stood face to face, separated by a window pane. We had switched places and now I was on the other side of the glass looking in at my old life with all of my things and my ex-fiancé behind her. I was shattered and could feel a deep wound in my chest as though I'd been pierced with a dagger in my heart. My anxiety went into overdrive; I was senseless for dismissing my intuition that had always known the truth. I was disgusted because we had continued to be intimate throughout our relationship - even on moving day. In a moment all of my suspicions that he was unfaithful and with who, were confirmed. Daisy was a known rival that had harassed and harmed me and she was instrumental in breaking up my home. She had provoked some of our most violent arguments to create problems that drove a wedge between us so that he'd continue running to her. But Aadi had brought her into my relationship, into my home and car. He'd gone further and manipulated me into giving him money and my belongings so they could setup a new life together. I had been humiliated for years; but the deception he created and the hate I felt was his to carry.

I felt disoriented and couldn't speak but the pain that registered across my face told him everything that I couldn't say. He came rushing out of the apartment door pulling his shirt on and I started sobbing. Aadi started pushing me very hard on my chest with the points of his fingers and as I stumbled back to gain my footing to keep from falling down, he continued pushing me harder. "Leave. Go! Go, now. You don't need to be seeing this," he said while adjusting his clothes. His actions didn't align with the feigned concern in his words. Daisy called the police and when she came out of the doorway she said, "I called the cops you fuckin' bitch." He turned his head toward her and when he looked back at me his tone changed and the look on his face became very angry. "Get the fuck out, go! You wanted it like this!" he yelled as he pointed in my face. He was playing both sides. "Aadi! What? Not like this! Not like this, Aadi!" I could barely find my words, I was crushed.

The officer arrived quickly and when he walked up from behind me, I collapsed from the grief of what was happening and I lunged forward and shoved Aadi screaming out that I hated him. The officer picked me up and carried me to the cruiser where I was handcuffed, arrested and put in jail. I never spoke to Aadi again.

I was heartbroken by what he had done and grieved for a year like someone had died. The person I knew as my best friend, whom I had fallen in love with, was long gone before we had even parted ways. I picked up the pieces of my shattered heart and moved forward into a new chapter of my life. I started going to the gym and lost all of the weight I'd gained and more within six months after the breakup and although I was sad, I felt a sense of relief that came from the freedom to blossom without being suppressed. My anxiety had gone away almost immediately but I couldn't date for a long time, I had a difficult time understanding how to trust myself with relationships going forward. I was later further humiliated by his lies when after our breakup I'd heard that he said I was an abusive cheater. I was astounded but I accepted how he felt or what he had to say about me because I knew the truth.

In a serendipitous moment many years later in September of 2015, I was driving into a shopping complex in Dublin, CA. It was late afternoon and as I drove in, I had to slow down to let a couple walk along in front of me in the crosswalk. I recognized them and Aadi looked up and to his right and we locked eyes while she kept her head down. I drove on after they passed and went about my shopping but when I returned to drive out twenty minutes later he was standing there alone. He stood at the end of the crosswalk and waited there for me to pass again. As I drove by I looked at him and I saw the look of sorrow and regret in his eyes and on his face but I continued to drive on. I could see in my rearview mirror that he looked on until I was almost out of view and then I saw him slowly turn and walk away. I had pushed the memory of him away and buried the pain but I had stayed with so much built up resentment for years. Up to this point, I'd forgotten about him and kept him in a lock box of painful memories that I stuffed down and didn't open. Our lives intersected once again at that crosswalk which was situated near the entrance of a restaurant that I had introduced him to and that we'd frequented for years. As I passed through the sliding doors it brought perspective and I saw that I had not missed out on anything and I didn't miss him, the lies and triangulation or the mundane relationship we had once shared. The distant memory of what had once been us could finally fade away.

10

THE COWORKER

A year after my separation from Aadi I started trying to navigate new relationships and I began seeing someone but he wanted to settle down very quickly and wanted to get married. I knew he wasn't the one so I broke it off. I'd met someone else that I was really interested in but after dating for several months he didn't seem to view us as a couple even though we were always together, I felt very used so I broke that off too. I started feeling empty and someone at work was paying a lot of attention to me and it piqued my curiosity and I began dating a married co-worker that pursued me relentlessly. He was very charming and he gave me a lot of attention; I was flattered when he flirted with me but he also flirted with everyone. I started to flirt back and things between us grew from there. JD was one of the new execs in our company and on his first day my department stood together to greet him and as the group of employees reached out their hands to shake his, he walked right by everybody and made a bee line for me. "Hi, how are you? I'm JD, it's nice to meet you," he said as he took my hand. I felt like time stood still when he and I met and I could feel my heart beating out of my chest. He was much older and for a brief time he was one of my bosses. As our relationship progressed I thought I had fallen in love with him but he was married and I wasn't going to ask him to be with me. He had told me that he was separated but still living with his ex while sorting out the details of their break up and I believed him because we openly dated for well past a year. He had a key to my place and we'd vacationed together - we had a relationship and I fell hard for him. Long after he and I had started dating, she had gotten angry and we got into a huge argument. She'd said things to me that indicated she was a bitter and that was trying to make me jealous. However, I noticed JD seemed to like it a little too much that she and I had quarreled over him and very soon afterward he told me that he was coming to a decision between the two of us. I immediately broke it off with him for good, I didn't realize that he was still very married to her because he was professing his love to me and we were spending a lot of time together.

I suddenly felt tremendous guilt for our relationship which now seemed to be reduced to nothing more than a fling. Both he and his wife made it extremely difficult for me to move on and although I felt I owed her an apology, I was very angry that neither of them was letting me move on and trying to keep me in the crosshairs of their failed relationship. I wanted nothing more to do with him and yet I dealt with her angry and harassing calls every day at my workplace. I made an inter-office transfer and began working in a new building and location but JD's wife phoned every day for months. One afternoon she phoned and in an effort to intimidate me said she wanted to speak with my boss. I put her on hold and my supervisor promptly took the call, listened to what she had to say and told her not to call my job again. While I was dealing with this constant harassment, JD on the other hand was stalking me. He was driving by my home, parking outside at all hours of the day and night. He didn't want me to break it off with him but I didn't want to stay. He'd show up in the parking lot at my college campus out of town where I was taking night classes or at other random places that I would be at because he was following me. I had fallen in love with JD but it was clearly an impossible relationship and this behavior was anything but loving. During one of our last conversations, he explained the reason for his wife's behavior but didn't say much about his own. He said that he'd dated someone else before me but that she seemed to hone her focus on me because she had once worked as his assistant and they had met under the same circumstances that we did. I could see that he had a pattern of how he found his wives and I didn't want to be his third. Regardless of how they met, I felt I owed her an apology because I knew exactly what it felt like to have your heart ripped out from betrayal and my selfish ways and ignorance weren't meant to hurt her but I did. I felt contrite for many years but I also knew that I wasn't the reason for their problems. I felt a very strong attachment to JD; I thought of him constantly and thought that I'd loved him. Maybe I did, but I also didn't know anything about trauma bonds at that time. I had to let him go and I felt sick and heartbroken over it.

Although he continued following me and continued to reach out to me from time to time, I didn't speak to him again until many years later. I would ignore him and he'd continue showing up at random places. He did this so often and for many years, it made me feel that he loved me and that he too was heartbroken; that perhaps I had made a mistake somehow in not saying enough or something more. But as I grew older I could see that he kept in touch to keep me attached and longing for him while he had no plans to change.

After I broke it off with JD, several months passed and I moved on from him and began dating someone new. Joe and I had a whirlwind romance, he was very special and loved me from the moment we said hello to each other. We met one day after I left my place for a much needed long drive to clear my mind. It was a beautiful spring morning and I put the convertible top down on my TT roadster and went for a long drive to clear my head. As the air whipped through my hair and the sun shined on my face, I decided to stop on a whim at the Porsche dealership in Marin County and that's where I met Joe. He thought I worked there but he and I were both browsing cars. It was just a nice day to stop and look I certainly couldn't afford to buy. Joe asked me to dinner that night, I went and we hit it off. After dating only a few weeks, he'd asked me to move in with him and I did. He surprised me after I moved in with a new Porsche and a month later we had plans to travel the world. I had quit my job at the phone company and we flew to our first stop in New York and Joe asked me to marry him. I wanted so desperately to feel that love but I couldn't, it was too much too soon and I didn't want to lead him on and he was heartbroken. I decided to cut the trip short and when we got back I gave him back the car and moved out. Our relationship was short lived but I was grateful for having met him and we stayed in touch for a while but eventually we both moved on.

My life and relationships were chaotic and messy. I needed to find another job and focus on me instead of love and dating.

11

NEW JOB

In the fall of 2006, I had met Mark at work when I had gotten hired as an Executive Assistant to the CMO for Zantaz – a software as a service company that was located in the East Bay Area of Northern California. I mostly found the company culture and environment to be very enjoyable and it was a fun and creative job where I felt appreciated. The atmosphere in my department was very laid back so much so that it was common to have Happy Hour in someone's office at the end of the day or whenever we needed a break from finishing up a big project. Everyone in my department had a mini-fridge at their desk and the champagne and bourbon were well-stocked. It was a fun place with many perks while working there such as game tables and daily refreshments for everyone to enjoy in the break room. I worked tirelessly around the clock and always came back the next day feeling happy to start my day. There was however a group of men that worked in the IT and Shipping Departments that had made me feel unwelcomed and uncomfortable from the moment I started my job. They were always rude and short tempered with me and it was in such contrast to how everyone else behaved. I mostly disregarded their harassing behavior but it exhausted me at times because it was intentional and I was singled out.

They'd taken to referring to me by disparaging names in an effort to insult my intelligence. Brian, the VP of the Shipping Department walked the premises like he owned the place and liked to intimidate and bully people. He took things too far when he came to my desk shouting at me for the entire floor to hear because he was upset about all of the mini-refrigerators that my department personnel had. We got into an argument when he stood over me and got into my face and I shouted back and told him to leave. His ego was bruised and he was very angry about not having control and he stormed off. That set the precedence for his behavior towards me during the majority of the time that I worked there. He wouldn't say anything more but he was passive-aggressive. He had been hired on through the CEO's assistant and he got away with mistreating people without consequence and most people coward to his tantrums because he had job security.

After that day, his personal friends that worked as IT helpdesk increased their attempts to undermine my work. When I placed orders or needed repairs done in the department, my requests went unanswered. When I posted helpdesk tickets in the queue they would get cancelled and closed. There were several challenges created to keep me from performing my job in an effort to sabotage me so that I would appear incompetent or frustrated enough to quit.

I didn't understand why they had taken such a dislike to me from the start but I had observed that they didn't treat others in the same way. Their harassing behavior was petty and immature and continued throughout the time I worked there so to work around it, I typically called on Mark directly. He worked as IT helpdesk personnel and he became the Marketing department go-to that was on speed dial.

I'd been working there only days when I had met Mark; he was called to fix an issue with my computer and as he sat at my desk trying to figure out the solution he didn't appear to look well. "Are you feeling ok?" I asked. "Oh, yes ma'am! Why do you ask?" I didn't want to catch the flu, the company had just given free flu shots out and people were getting sick. Although Mark was a little older than me he had a polite way of addressing everyone that was reminiscent of his southern roots and I detected a slight inflection when he spoke. It was cute and charming. "Because you're shaking and you look flushed and appear to be sweating," I said. "Oh, yes ma'am. I'm sorry, I'm just trying to sort out this technical issue and it's taking a while; I'm keeping you from your work," he said while looking straight ahead at the computer. "Not at all, my apologies if I'm making you anxious - let me leave you to it so that I'm not standing over you and breathing down your neck. Actually, I have other things to take care of and I'll be back in an hour. Is that enough time for you?" I asked as I looked at my watch. "Yes ma'am, I'm sorry. I'll have this sorted out for you and have you ready to go in no time. You can come back much sooner if you'd like, I appreciate you being patient with me." It was a noisy area and I was happy to leave for a short while but when I arrived back at my desk an hour later, Mark was still working through the technical issues. Roy, a co-worker in the engineering department, walked over and moved him out of the way and resolved my computer issue within minutes. Roy said, "See Mark, that literally took five minutes and I'm not even IT helpdesk. I don't know what you were doing, man. It's almost as if you don't know how to do your job."

Roy looked at me and said, "Yolanda, Mark can't concentrate because it's *your* computer. Don't worry Mark, I came to her rescue man. You can go now. Go catch your breath." Roy stood up and broke into a big grin while he and another work mate, Gino, snickered. It was an interesting first introduction to meeting Mark and the guys were giving him a hard time. Mark looked sheepish and I felt sorry for him but he was always on call for me anytime my department needed work done from the IT department going forward.

Mark is tall with a naturally muscular build and his polite southern manners stand out. He knows how to be charming and when to be coy, especially with the ladies. I thought he was such a nice guy and after that day I had gotten used to seeing him most days at work while making small talk and listening to his stories of plight in navigating life as a single Dad with an infant. I worked there for seven months before the company was purchased by Autonomy and in May 2007, the Marketing department was laid-off. At the end of my last work day I invited him to join me at a local pub and grill up the street where my coworkers were gathering for a final farewell. He came to see me off and we kept in touch afterward and started seeing each other.

12

THE ROOMMATE

Soon after I had started working at Zantaz I answered an ad for a room vacancy and made a difficult decision to move from my apartment because I needed to pay off debt. I had a large debt and to pay it quickly I rented a room so that I could be in another place in six months without juggling bills. Susan owned a condo in a gated community up the street from my apartment in the suburbs of San Ramon, CA and I met her when I answered her ad for a roommate and afterward stopped by to look at her place. Moving was tiresome and emotionally difficult for me especially because I'd done it twice in a short few months' time and now this would be a third and most of my things would be placed in storage. Weeks after moving in she told me that she was awaiting a sentencing for DUI charges and that she was also newly pregnant. I was shocked at her news and angry that I had been misled into renting out her room without being allowed to make a more informed decision, given her life circumstances. I contemplated moving out but I was dealing with several life changes at once and I felt overwhelmed. Susan's circumstances were peculiar and cause for alarm but I decided to stay because I spent an infrequent amount of time there and she mostly stayed with her boyfriend (who lived 1 minute away in the same condo community). I didn't stay mad long and felt a deep sadness for her when she told me that her mother had recently passed away. As time went on, I recognized that there were many red flags from the start while living with Susan that put her behavior and motives into question; if only I had followed my instincts and moved out sooner, things would have ended so differently.

Soon after announcing her criminal charges and pregnancy news, Susan took to washing and drying all of my laundry. She ruined clothes that were made of materials clearly meant to be dry cleaned and seemed oblivious that my skirts and shirts were shrunken to the point of looking like child wear but when I asked her to stop, it continued and she seemed to have no semblance of her intrusiveness. The laundry area in the hallway faced my bathroom and I would come in from work and find the hamper empty with my clothes folded on my bathroom counter. One night I found a freshly laundered clothing pile was sitting on my bed as I came in from work and I went back into the living room to talk to her. "Oh, wow, you're still doing my laundry and you've been in my room. Thanks…I really appreciate your help but you don't have to keep doing it," I told her. "That's ok hon, I'm here doing mine and you're always working and never around. Like I've said before I'm just trying to help you out, hon." "Really, I don't expect you to do it and most all of it needs to be dry cleaned and pressed anyway. I haven't taken anything in for a while because I haven't gotten around to it, besides I have so many other clothes that I can wear. I'm also allergic to your detergent and can't wear scented laundry soap. But seriously, you don't have to do it and I'd prefer that you didn't" I said. "Yeah I know, I've been in your room and I've looked around," she said. "The first time I opened the door and looked inside I said, 'Holy shit, what the fuck?!' this girl has so much stuff! It could take days for me to look through everything; it's like a clothing store. Your room is like a closet, you have so much fucking stuff, I swear to god," she said while shaking her head in disbelief. "I used your detergent, hon. You must be allergic to the fabric softener. You're allergic to Snuggles? I promise that I only put in just a really small capful. Promise. Just a really itty bitty tiny capful," she said as she switched to a baby voice and made a small pinching motion with her fingers. I was caught by surprise that she'd been in my room and the look on my face registered anger but before I could say anything she continued in her baby voice and quickly said, "I promise I don't touch anything besides your laundry, I just go in there and look around. You have so many things to look at that I like to stand in there looking at everything." The conversation was tense and uncomfortable but I got the impression that she understood without my having to repeat it that she was to stop doing my laundry and going into my room. I was pissed off and I walked away towards my room, closing and locking the door behind me. I did some work from my laptop and went to sleep.

After another few weeks went by I came into my room at the end of my work day to find a pile of my clothes had been dry cleaned and neatly laid on my bed along with a dress that I didn't recognize. I was furious that she continued violating my boundaries and I couldn't confront her in the moment because she wasn't present. I wanted to speak to her in person and I waited until the day came that we were in the condo at the same time. She was costing me money and her attempts to appear helpful were doing more harm than good, and she was being deliberately obtuse. I'd been living there for a handful of months now and I usually saw her once a week as we passed each other, but I waited nearly two weeks before getting the chance to talk with her. When she came to the condo as the weekend was approaching I'd noticed something looked differently about her but my thoughts were focused on speaking with her about my laundry. "Susan, thank you for dry cleaning my clothes. Girl, you have to stop," I said. "What do you mean?" she asked. "Stop with the laundry and the dry cleaning. I appreciate that you're trying to be helpful but I don't need you doing it and stop going into my room. I've been thinking about moving out, so..." "Oh, yeah? Why hon? I'm barely here, why would you think of doing that? I'm still waiting to hear but if I'm sentenced to jail they're saying I might be gone a year. Can you believe it? God, fuck! Fuck, shit!" she said while throwing her hands in the air. "You'll have the place to yourself if you want to stay and continue paying just for your room. My court date is soon and when I get back I'm moving in with Bill and we're going to raise Baby together at his place," she continued.

She had no shortage of dramatic events unfolding in her life and I'd noticed that she used her plight to manipulate and evoke sympathy at every turn, especially to divert attention away from conversations she didn't want to have. It worked and in the moment I quickly lost sight of the dry cleaning and we began talking about her upcoming court case. She started crying and telling me how scared she was and that she missed her mom, I felt so awful for her that I gave her a hug and insisted I pay her back for the dry cleaning. As she spoke she placed her hand on her stomach and I could see that her belly was starting to show. While she continued talking she opened the door to the balcony and stood outside while she lit a cigarette – the same skinny cigarettes that I smoked. As she sat down on the bench outside, a plume of smoke encircled her and as the light of the porch lamp shone directly on her head I'd noticed that she had colored her hair from her mostly grey dirty-blonde hair, to a similar dark brown color that I had. I was no longer listening and my mind drifted in thought to the maniacal character in a 90's movie about roommates. Up to this point, I had been telling my friends and a few coworkers about her crazy behavior and life and they had heard all about the laundry situation. But they all laughed it off and dismissed it, saying they wished they had my problems of coming home to someone having done their laundry. I quickly felt bad for thinking that she could be anything close to resembling that crazy character and snapped back to reality. She took a long drag of her Virginia Slim and then said, "Oh by the way hon, I put a dress in your room. It's one of mine and it's old but I only wore it a couple of times. I haven't been able to wear it for years and there's no way I'll ever be able to wear it again." The cigarette smoke was thick and surrounded her. "It would look so good on your cute figure, you can have it. Go try it on," she said. "I saw that. It's not really my style but thank you anyway, you can keep it," I said. It was clear that she was struggling with major interpersonal difficulties. The following morning the smell of bacon was wafting throughout the condo and woke me up. I realized Susan hadn't gone to her boyfriends the night before and I checked the clock and saw that it read almost 8am. I wanted to sleep in but that was impossible now and instead I got up and dressed and as I was heading out the front door she called out from the kitchen and said, "Where are you going, hon? Come sit down, I made breakfast." "Oh, no thanks, I've got to run," I said. "But I made extra. I even put peppers and sausage in the eggs with lots of cheese and there's bacon too. Let me get you some juice while you help yourself, the plates are over here," she said, pointing to the kitchen cabinets. "No thank you, I'm not hungry and I'm on my way out. I'll grab a slice of bacon but you didn't have to cook anything for me," I said. I quickly grabbed a slice of bacon and went out the door. I didn't see her for the remainder of the weekend and on that following Monday she sent a plant delivery to my work and while my coworkers found the gesture to be friendly and thoughtful, I found it disturbing. I threw the plant away and an uneventful few months rolled by. While I kept very busy with work an announcement was made of our company buy-out by Autonomy and lay-offs happened quickly. I filed for unemployment the following Monday and had left my paperwork sitting in the kitchen that Sunday night because Susan was usually at her boyfriends those evenings. At some point she came to the condo and had taken my unemployment filing to fax it "as a favor" to me she'd later said. I was angry but she said she was trying to be helpful. She was set to begin her yearlong jail term and she would have her baby while incarcerated – I felt so much sorrow for her. We'd come to a favorable arrangement where we agreed that I would look after her place and begin renting her condo as my own after she was released from jail. She'd be remanded to Bill's to serve several additional months on house arrest and she was scheduled to serve her jail time soon. I wouldn't see her at the condo for a long while which would be a welcomed relief.

13

THE SHOE BOX

I stayed at the pub and grill for an hour to say goodbye to everyone after my last day of work at Zantaz and had invited Mark to come over to my place later that evening. I'd mentioned when I got in that he was coming over and Susan eagerly waited around to meet him like a nosey neighbor. "Where the fuck's he at already?!" she asked briskly with a hint of irritation in her tone. "He said he was going to be here by 8pm, he didn't even eat dinner with you!" she continued. "So? He's busy, he has a kid and I'm not worried about the time. Why aren't you at Bill's?" I asked. "Because! You haven't dated anyone since you've lived here and I wanna meet this guy. I wanna know who he is and what he looks like!" she exclaimed. I never spoke to her about my romantic life and let her assume but my current living arrangement wasn't exactly ideal for a relationship. With her being gone soon and for quite a while, that would all change. Her life was like watching an episode of Jerry Springer and by this time I'd grown familiar to her crass and raunchy behavior and outlandish stories. Her strange behavior reminded me a lot of my brother. When he wasn't angry he would say inappropriate or odd things and behave strangely; it would make everyone uncomfortable but you lived with it and learned to ignore it. Susan worked mostly with men and she'd spoken often in frustration of her lackluster sex life with Bill and before Mark arrived she told me about a peculiar encounter that she'd had at work with an international client that was in town on business. "Oh my god, so after the meeting was over you stayed behind in the conference room talking with him and just flashed him your boobs?" I was dumbfounded at what she'd told me. "Without hesitation, just like that? One moment it's all business and then you have your shirt up?" I asked in astonishment. "Yeah, I closed the door after the meeting and everyone left and I turned around and walked right up to him and went like this!" she said as she proceeded to flash her breasts. "What did he do?" I asked. "He reached out and touched them and I forced him to grab on 'em! And then he started sucking one of my tits." she said as she made a gesture as though sucking a bottle. She's so crass, I thought, as she broke into a raucous laughter. "What do you think he did? He had tits in his face!" she said in amusement as she crossed her eyes and held her hand before her nose. She was very strange. "Oh my god girl, you need to go home to Bill's and take a cold shower. I can't believe you did that". I waited for the punch line, thinking she was joking but she was serious and kept laughing until tears streamed down her face. While she kept herself amused all I could think was that she craved attention in strange ways and that her behavior was bizarre and she seemed disturbed; but the rent on the room was cheap and she wasn't always there.

I heard a knock at the door and knew Mark had arrived. Although Susan and I were only roommates, I made an effort to be polite and introduced them as I invited him in. He reached to shake Susan's hand and I observed how her body language shifted and her eyes widened as she studied and drank him in. His charismatic and gracious nature was in such contrast to her own; I sensed her intrigue and immediate attraction to him and wanted her to leave but it was still her place so I didn't ask her to. I grabbed his hand and we walked to my room as I called out from the hallway for her to have a goodnight so that she'd take the hint and go. We heard Susan leave soon and afterward I proceeded to tell him all about her while he listened in disbelief. I'd gotten used to seeing him at work every day and he felt comfortable and familiar to me, I liked having him there and I wanted a security blanket. As he sat across from me on my bed and patiently listened to me go on about why I still lived there, I could see the attraction in his gaze and he and I began seeing each other after that night.

He came over one evening at the end of his work shift with a shoebox filled with cell phones. He'd previously mentioned in passing that he had been visiting with former employees during his work day at their homes; he was retrieving work cell phones that they had kept and continued to use after they had been laid off. I found it odd that he'd been asked to retrieve them because the company had been generous to their employees and I clearly remembered that when the layoffs began all executives were allowed to keep their cell phone and laptop; I too was gifted them by my superior on my last day but my line had shutoff when my employment ended. "What's in the box, did you get new shoes?" I asked. "No, look. These are all those cell phones I'd been picking up from everyone. They were put in the dumpster and I kept 'em. This one here is Gabriela's phone. You remember her?" he asked as he picked up one of the phones. "She's such a nice lady, I was at her house talking with her for a long time." he continued. "You just dove into the dumpster and grabbed those out? How did you know they were in there...were you dumpster diving at work?" I asked jokingly. "I didn't actually go *into* the dumpster, I was throwing 'em away outside and decided to keep them and put 'em in my car. Don told me to throw 'em out," he said. "Why did you have to go out of your way to collect them in the first place just to throw them out? What are you going to use them for?" I asked. "I'm gonna sell them. I can get at least a hundred for each of 'em. The company just wanted me to get 'em back but the employees want new ones so these won't be getting issued to anyone," he said. "I think you should ask Don if it's ok that you keep them. I mean, if he told you to throw them away then it's still company property unless he says you can have them." I said. "Oh, Don won't have a problem with it, trust me. He already told me to throw 'em away. He said to just get rid of them. But to be sure, I will ask him again…just for you," he said as he smiled and leaned down and pecked my lips. Don stayed on as VP IT when Autonomy bought Zantaz and the next day Mark told me that Don said he could have them. I didn't have any reason to doubt him and I believed him because while I had worked there the V.P.'s had hiring and firing capability so if Don told him it was ok, it seemed that it was. I also remembered that the Shipping and IT departments made their own rules without being questioned and although it seemed like an unconventional way of doing business, the 'higher ups' and rest of the company allowed it. It appeared that the company was still functioning per usual even though they were now owned by Autonomy but that didn't seem unusual either because some of the C-line executives between the two companies knew each other. In the following days Mark sold several of the phones and asked if I could also help him create an ad to sell the rest online.

I didn't want to go back to an office job any longer and I started a new spray tanning business. Through business networking I met a local group of women and began working with them as a makeup artist. My calendar started filling up quickly and several days out of the week I worked long hours from the early evenings and late into the night. My new schedule was getting hectic and it didn't leave much time for Mark and I to spend with each other since he also shared custody of his child. I was busy with my life and Mark and I saw each other when we could and kept in touch regularly but I otherwise didn't know what was going on in his daily life at work or at home.

Susan was getting her affairs aligned as the start of her sentence was looming near and I met with her for dinner at a local restaurant. She wanted to go over the details about staying in the condo and asked me to help water a few plants and said that she'd send Bill over to pick up the rent each month. When we arrived at the local restaurant I met Max, her friend and neighbor that lived next door to the condo. He came in with his wife and Susan quickly introduced us as they briefly stopped to say hello and were seated nearby. While we continued eating our waitress brought a beer to our table and said it had been paid for and pointed in Max's direction. I raised the beer to say thank you and Susan immediately flashed a scowl in his direction and got angry. She looked at my beer and said, "What? What the fuck is that?" She scoffed as she continued to stare at my drink. "What do you mean?" I asked as I casually chugged my cold beer. "Fuck! He's just sending over drinks to you?" I could hear the jealousy and suspicion dripping in her tone and her face flushed red in anger. "Well he's your friend and neighbor; I think he's just trying to be nice considering I'm their neighbor now too. If you want a beer or something else then ask him to buy you one. What are you, mad?" Her scowl quickly shifted to surprise at what I'd said and she seemed to calm down enough to finish eating her dinner. I was only half way through my beer but I was ready to go. I asked for my check and when the waitress came back she brought my check along with another beer to the table and placed it before me. I moved it toward Susan thinking it was hers and the waitress moved it back and said it was another for me. "What? What the fuck is this? I'm sitting right here!" she shouted and pouted. I turned around to raise my bottle once again in thanks and yelled out, "Hey Max, thank you so much to the both of you for the beers but you better get your neighbor a Coke because she's about to lose it over here!" We all laughed and he said, "Oh yeah, sure. Sorry about that Sue". I signed my check and left, she followed me out and had stayed angry at Max. While we walked to the parking lot she told me that they'd been friends for over twenty years and I gathered by her reaction at the restaurant that it appeared there may have been more to her friendly feelings than she let on. I was looking forward to having the place to myself after she was gone.

14

BULLSHIT RADAR

Susan was gone. She had gone to jail and she came back out to deliver her baby and had a brief hospital stay and went back inside. Bill knew where she was but she didn't tell anyone else and webbed a story for her friends and family and took a leave of absence from her job so that it aligned with her delivery and no one would know. It had been several months since I had been laid off and I was working hard at trying to get my business going and I was still working on the photo shoots with the other girls. The economic crash of 2008 unfolded and the world was in the midst of a financial meltdown and it was so frightening. Mark and I were having problems and I didn't want to see him anymore. I went to lunch with my dear friend Graham; we had known each other for a few years and had once dated but we remained good friends and we frequently socialized. Clark is a self-made wealthy businessman and he grew up scrapping on the inner city streets of the Bay Area, he is both equal parts business savvy and street smarts. I often confided in him and he always looked out for me and gave me sage advice. He had met Mark and didn't like him from the start. I noticed most men didn't like Mark and that it appeared that he didn't have any friends; aside from his child, his extended family was in Greenville,

South Carolina. Graham had a strong bullshit radar but out of respect to me he was always very friendly to Mark the few times I brought him to dine with us. Graham felt he was using me and pointed out that we had nothing in common and didn't hold back when he listed off the many other ways that we were incompatible. I knew Graham was right, Mark and I had been seeing each other for months but we didn't have anything in common and we never did anything but hang out and have sex. I'd known early on that it wasn't a great fit for a long term relationship yet I still continued seeing him. I made excuses to Graham and side-stepped having the conversation when it came up again because I knew the relationship was a dead-end and I wasn't doing much to change it. "You're not yourself, this guy isn't good for you," Graham said while eating a forkful of his chicken Cobb salad. Here we go again, I thought. "Why do you keep saying that? My god, stop. I'm not eating now." I said as I pushed my plate away. "What, what are you doing? Eat your food," he said while extending his palm out. "I keep telling you it's not a relationship, it's just sex." I said as I rolled my eyes and drank the last sip of my cosmopolitan. I'd said that a little too loudly and had caught the attention of the waitress so I signaled her for another drink. "Can you bring me another Cosmo, please? Bombay Sapphire? Thank you!" I was exasperated that this conversation was coming up again, but I knew Graham was only looking out for me. "You're ordering a second drink at lunch? I didn't think you should've ordered the first one. It's the middle of the day," he said as he raised his eyebrows in disapproval and went back to eating his salad. He could be very intense at times and today was one of those days. "You're giving me anxiety. I thought we were going to eat and have a nice time and now you're giving me a lecture and stressing me out." I said. "Look, I'm telling you. I've been telling you – he's bad news and he's using you. I can spot that shit from a mile away man. He's got much more to gain by being with you than the other way around, that's for sure". I stayed silent while picking at my salad with my fork. "Why are you acting blind to this? Look at you - ambitious, smart, holding it down for yourself, fuckin' beautiful. You got a lot to offer a man and from what you've told me he makes decent money; and he's struggling to pay his bills? This guy really knows how to tug at your heart strings and has you feeling badly for him all the time. Sounds like he needs his mother. He's really the lucky man you choose? He does nothing for you, absolutely fuckin' nothing and he never takes you anywhere. The guy's a deadbeat. He did what – oh, that's right, he bought you one bouquet of roses way back when on one of your first dates." he said mockingly. I looked up at him. "That's right, I remembered, I don't forget anything. Has he done anything else for you? No. He takes from you," he said. "He has a kid he takes care of," I said quietly. Graham smirked and leaned forward putting his hand behind his ear and said, "Wait, what? Excuse me? I didn't hear you. This is mind boggling! Are you fuckin' serious? He told you that he fought for shared custody because he didn't want to pay child support, Yolanda". I couldn't say a word, Graham was right. I continued to stay silent and the heat from the embarrassment I felt was rising to my face. "He lives in the 'hood…don't give me that look, all I'm saying is I know the neighborhood well and I can assure you the rent is cheap there," he continued. "What did he say he was making again? 75- 85 a year, during *this* economy? Hmph. Well if that's true it ain't chump change, where's his money going? What's with this cell phone business? He doesn't know how to treat you. He's irresponsible financially and otherwise and he's using you, he's a total fuckin' deadbeat. Just tell me something - what the fuck is that? What are you doing? You've had a lot more. You deserve a lot more, you know you do". Graham stared straight at me gesturing with his hands that he was waiting for a response, but I was on the verge of tears with nothing to say and stared down at my fork. Clark is older than me by twenty five years and I felt like I just got lectured by my dad. I couldn't explain why I was putting up with Mark because things had changed between us. We were going through some major problems. He'd recently tried to run me over in his car after we had a petty disagreement. While we were out of town doing some shopping we'd gotten into an argument over something he misunderstood and he told me to fuck off and left the store and didn't return. When I went to find him I saw that his car was gone from the parking lot and that he had left me stranded a half an hour away from my home and my purse was in his car. Fortunately I had my cell phone because I didn't know anyone's number by memory or money for a taxi. My friend Carol brought me home and as we pulled up Mark was leaving my condo with some of his belongings. I was furious that he had left me stranded and that he had been in my home without my permission and when I got out of Carol's car, I stepped in front of his and was yelling at him so that he wouldn't drive away. He looked at me in a moment of hesitation and then pressed on the gas and almost ran me over. I didn't have time to move out of the way and jumped up to keep from being run down and I landed on the hood. As he drove he swerved to throw me off and I rolled off and landed on my feet. Carol had asked me if I was ok and if I wanted her to call the police but I had told her no. Mark called later and told me that he didn't see me standing there and thought I had jumped on his car, that I'd scared him so he then took off. He swore that was how it happened and had a complete melt down because I wouldn't believe him. He was adamant that I had jumped on his car and wouldn't address anything else. The conversation exhausted me and he was adamant about how his perception of what happened was the truth; I started to feel unsure. If Graham knew this had happened, there was no way I could explain why I had allowed Mark back into my life. "This guy is why you're depressed," Graham continued. "Fuck 'it's the economy' bullshit, this guy is why you're depressed *and* you need to move too. You know this. You can't hang around someone or people who are lazy and have no ambition and not expect that it won't drive you fuckin' nuts or rub off on you," Graham said as he sat there with the stack of bills in his hand that he pulled from the inside of his jacket. He had a point; he had made several points clear. Mark was content with no goals or plans for his future and it bothered me to no end that he was so lazy. We didn't see life in the same way. And separately, I didn't like Susan, like living with her or how she was living; she was strange and I knew I needed to move. "I know. You're right, you're right." I said. "But I don't want to talk about this anymore, let's just talk about something else. I'm tired now." I said as I picked at my blackened salmon caesar. It was my favorite and I always ordered it when we came to the grille in Blackhawk. But I wasn't in the mood to eat my salad and I placed my elbow on the table and rested my forehead in my hand. "Are you eating or am I boxing this for you to take?" he asked. "I'm not eating, I'm still sulking." I said. "Incredible. I'll get a box. Dammit, it's going to leave a smell in the DB9. We're not taking that. When she comes back I'm paying the bill and sending back that drink. I have something I need to do in Walnut Creek later, but let's go to the Broadway Plaza there and kill some time. Come on, smile. I'll buy you some shoes," he said with a grin. I perked up, I love shoes. "Oh, I almost forgot – I made you an appointment for next week to see a doctor. Go to the appointment and talk to him, it's paid for." Graham said.

The following week, I went to my appointment and left with a prescription for anti-depressants to help me lift my mood and control the anxiety I was feeling. I had been worried about the economy amongst other things but so far work continued and I was grateful but I was stressed out. Immediately after I started taking my anti-depressants I noticed within days that I started having erratic behavior and extremely heightened anxiety; I didn't feel better but worse. My new doctor quickly changed the dosage because of the side effects but it went on for several months while one side-effect calmed and another surfaced so he put me on a different prescription but nothing changed. I decided to stop taking them because I didn't have any improvements but instead felt worse.

Susan was gone for several months and when she was remanded to house arrest she had officially moved out by putting most of her things in the garage and taking the rest with her; afterward I began renting her condo from her. Finally I'd be renting my own place again and I wouldn't have to see or speak with her aside from paying the rent.

15

RETURN TO ZANTAZ

Mark and I were back to getting along. Aside from the incident with the car, I still continued to see him a few times each week. He was usually extremely nice and was always actively attentive to me just as he had been when we'd met and worked together. It was more so now that we weren't working together, it was as though he studied me closely. For example, many times I'd wake up to him staring at me. If I finished my water, he was paying attention and would have another at the ready in the moment I took my last sip. If I dropped something he would race in that very second to pick it up and hand it to me with a kiss. If he'd spent the night he played with my hair until I fell asleep and he always kissed me goodbye each morning as I slept. He was very attentive; at times it felt almost a little too much. I had a painting party with family and friends and he was very generous with his time and effort and helped us paint the condo, everyone thought he was great and he worked tirelessly to help me. When we had finished it looked like a new place and I was pleased to have a new start again. He had brought up concerns with some activity that was going on in his apartment complex and I was letting him stay over more often while he looked for a new place. One morning in April 2009, he had stayed the night and before he left to work he bent down and gave me a kiss goodbye. I had fallen back to sleep when he came rushing in a couple of hours later. He had barged in and slammed the door and came into my room yelling and shouting that he had just gotten fired as he stood there panting and out of breath. I was confused and was trying to make sense of what was happening. "You fucking scared me! What the FUCK is wrong with you?" I yelled. "Sorry, I'm sorry. I didn't mean to. I'm the one who's scared!" he said. "What are you talking about? What happened, what's going on?" I asked with irritation in my tone. I was immediately peeved with how he stormed into my place and startled me; he could've been badly hurt. "I got fired! They said I stole some stuff. But I didn't do anything and they called a meeting and when I went in there they started asking me a buncha questions and they fired me," he said. "What did they ask you?" I was sitting up in bed rubbing my eyes and trying to calm down. "They were asking about those phones I recently got; you remember those phones I took back?" he asked. "Yes." I said. "Yeah, those. Well, they didn't get 'em. The phone company said they didn't get 'em and now they're saying I stole them" he said. "What do you mean? Are you talking about those new phones in boxes? I thought you bought them and had permission to get those?" I asked. Mark had been selling new cell phones that had their packaging and when I asked how he'd gotten them he said he'd had permission to buy them through the company on a discount. I found that unusual and when I had pressed him about it he maintained that he had permission and was submitting expense reports for them. I didn't believe him and he later showed me one of his reports that he submitted every month that Don had helped finish and had instructed him to submit to a woman in accounting. Mark referred to her by first name because I had known who she was while I had worked there and she had stayed on after the buyout. Like the phones from the shoebox, he had asked me to help him place some ads to sell his phones and I had helped him on a few occasions. He had recently ordered a large amount of phones and had said that he was sending them back because he wasn't allowed to have ordered that many at once. It seemed unusual but it appeared that he had permission. "I did. Don said it was ok. But this other guy started asking me about them and the spreadsheets that Don helped me do, and a bunch of other stuff," he said. "They fired me and now I don't know what to do," he said. "If you have permission from Don then what's the big deal? He's the VP of IT. You should call him if he wasn't the one you had the meeting with and try to resolve what's going on." I said. "Look, I'm tired. I'm pissed that you barged into my house like that so I'm going back to bed. Go call your supervisor, I'm sure it will all get sorted out," I said. "You're right, I'm sorry I came into your home like that I didn't mean to scare you, I'll go call Don," he said and came forward to peck me on the cheek and left. When I heard the front door close I immediately felt guilty for not handling his bad news in a more supportive way, he obviously needed someone to talk to and seemed scared. He seemed to be going through a lot in recent weeks with looking for a new place and now getting fired, I thought.

After he left I couldn't go back to sleep and called him to come back over to hang out. While he was at my place, Don phoned his cell and asked him to drop off his telecommuting equipment at the work place by the morning. I guess it didn't get resolved, I thought. He was expected to sign off on paperwork to demonstrate he returned his company issued items and Don instructed him to place labels on everything with 'Return to Zantaz' because he wasn't allowed back inside. When Mark hung up the phone he looked frightened but I tried my best to put him at ease and mentioned that when he saw Don he needed to talk with him in person and find out what was going on so that he could go back into work; that there was clearly some type of mistake that had been made and that things could get sorted out. While talking to Mark I filled out a pad of sticky notes for him with 'Return to Zantaz'. That's weird I thought, the company is now called Autonomy. I finished writing and handed the pad to him while he continued talking. When he'd asked me if he could borrow my car because mine had more room in it to gather his belongings, I didn't hesitate to help him out and he left to collect his things. He wanted to drop them off immediately and not wait until the morning and when he returned a couple of hours later, he was unusually quiet and said that Don wasn't answering his calls anymore. He didn't feel comfortable leaving his things at the door without speaking to someone and I encouraged him to try again in the morning. Meanwhile, I asked him to remove his things from my car and to go home to relax because I had plans for that evening and needed my car back. While in the middle of our conversation Susan's house phone rang, she wasn't living there anymore but the phone never rang; so I answered it. It was Susan calling from Bill's and she said, "The cops are on their way over to my place." She and Bill lived a quick 1 minute drive from my door and while he was working long hours and gone for most of the day, she'd been slipping off her ankle bracelet and showing up unannounced for a few minutes on occasion. She had timed that she could remove her bracelet for a set amount of minutes before her device alerted the authorities. They'd already been to her place once to check on her and to tighten her ankle device so when she phoned me and said that the police were on their way to her place, I assumed she had been caught. Everyone was coming to me with their problems today, I thought. I responded by asking her what she was going to do and she clarified that she wasn't speaking about Bill's place but about her place –

the condo that I was living in and that the police were looking for Mark. I was baffled and asked her why the police were calling her to tell me they looking for him but she started stammering and said they'd be there any minute and offered no further explanation. I hung up and was livid about the phone call and I told Mark that I didn't want his problems at my house and that the police were on their way to my home looking for him. I demanded that he explain at once why the police were searching for him. "I don't know, Yolanda I didn't do anything wrong! I don't know why the cops are looking for me!" he said. Mark continued to proclaim he had done nothing wrong and I wasn't sure what to believe and as the tension grew in the few minutes before they arrived I was caught by surprise when it looked as though he were about to cry. "Ok, ok, calm down. I believe you," I said. I hugged him and tried to console him and told him to stay calm. They had arrived and he went outside to speak with them but he came in after several minutes; he was being arrested because his job said that he had stolen equipment and he came back inside to let me know that they were going to take his items from my car. Mark looked like he had been crying and I felt awful for him. "I'm really worried. I don't know what I'm gonna do," he said. "Look, don't worry. I know that getting fired and accused of stealing has you scared but you know you didn't do anything wrong. Call me in the morning or when you can and let me know what's going on," I said. Mark gave me a big hug and said thank you while he kissed my cheek and walked out of the door. He phoned me in the morning and he asked if I could bail him out and said that he'd pay me back when he was released and I did. When I picked him up he hadn't slept all night and looked awful; the poor guy was a wreck.

I resumed my schedule and went about my life and a few days later Susan asked me to move out. I had barely just finished painting the condo and I felt Susan used Mark's arrest as an excuse. I'd asked her why the police had called her but she didn't give a direct answer but then said that she was going through a lot of problems of her own and didn't want any trouble because she was on house arrest. I understood but it still didn't answer why they were calling her. I very quickly found another place and she and I agreed that she'd refund the remainder of my rent and my deposit but after I moved out she didn't send anything and claimed I put spray tan on her walls and that my two kittens peed all over her carpets. None of that was true and the kitties came to me already having been potty trained. She and I were no longer on good terms now that she kept my money. In the recent weeks leading up to Mark's arrest she had been behaving strangely and asking inappropriate questions about my sex life with Mark that I ignored. She also seemed resentful and appeared passive-aggressive. Her behavior gave me the impression that she felt resentful in some way, and I surmised it was because I wasn't living with the concerns she faced while I stayed on living untroubled in her condo as she stayed shackled on house arrest and with a boyfriend she didn't seem happy with. He kept asking her to marry him she'd said but I knew from what he'd told me that he had put her in jail. He told me about their altercation one day when I saw him outside collecting her mail from the mailbox. I felt Susan had taken an opportunity to ask me to leave for many reasons but now that her condo looked more appealing with fresh paint and new window treatments, it could also rent for much more. And it eventually did. If it hadn't been the incident with Mark being arrested there would have been a different excuse and I was ready to move on.

16

YOU'VE BEEN SERVED

Moving day arrived and Mark and two acquaintances of mine helped me move. Mark's lease was expiring and he was now unemployed and really concerned about how he was going to manage. He was certain that he'd find new employment but he still didn't feel safe at his studio apartment. Even though I had been evicted because of him, I didn't lay the blame entirely on him because of how Susan was behaving. I felt bad for everything that he was going through and I believed he was innocent and I didn't want to see him homeless. I had a furnished spare room and invited him to live with me for a short time while he was getting himself back on his feet and continuing to look for a new place. I wasn't keen on living with children and Mark said he understood and that most times when he had his child, he made sleepover arrangements with his babysitter because his child liked being with their kids. He agreed to pay half of the rent and continued to thank me for my help. Inviting Mark to stay in my home was complicated for me because I liked living alone and we weren't an actual couple but I was comfortable with him and was open to helping him out for a small time. I had been seeing him for two years but I didn't call him my boyfriend. He hadn't officially met both of my parents but had met my mom when she was over and I had introduced him to Graham but he had otherwise only met a few of my other friends on rare occasion. He wasn't a part of my life as a boyfriend and I was feeling apprehensive and communicated my feelings to Mark and I was relieved that he seemed understanding. We agreed that if things didn't work out that he would move out.

He sold his bedroom furniture to an acquaintance of mine and he moved into my spare bedroom with just his clothes. After Mark moved in I contacted my landlord and told him that he was staying with me but my landlord insisted that he be on my lease agreement because he was an adult, the alternative was that he had to move out. My next door neighbor knew my landlord and he knew Mark was there so I couldn't allow him to stay. I spoke with Mark and he looked scared because he was going to have to move. He didn't have family nearby and although he only had his clothes to pack, he said he didn't have anywhere to go. I had an uncle who was also named Mark and he died a young man in his thirties while alone and homeless in a park. I knew that Mark couldn't qualify for another place live until he had a job and I was reluctant to allow him on my lease agreement but I didn't want to kick him out onto the street. What could go wrong? He was looking for a new job and would continue to look for a new place soon. If it didn't work out here, we had agreed that I would communicate that and he'd move out.

In the early evening a few weeks later, someone was urgently knocking at my door. I hurried to the door and when I opened it a man asked me, "Are you Yolanda?" "Yes." "Is Mark here?" he asked. "Mark!" I called out. "Who are you? How did you get past the security guard?" I asked. A large envelope was shoved into each of mine and Mark's hands and the man said, "You've been served. Sorry about that guys, I'm just the messenger."

It was May 2009 and I was being served a lawsuit by my former employer, Zantaz. I was completely confused. They were also suing Mark and several other men for fraud. Aside from Mark, I hadn't seen or spoken to anyone after being laid off with the majority of the company two years prior. I was shocked that I was being sued but more so because Zantaz had been bought by Autonomy when I left in May 2007. I saw the list of defendants and remembered most of the men very well because they were the bullies that worked in the IT and Shipping departments and Mark had said they had stayed on with the new company after the merger. I contacted an attorney and I wanted to respond but he explained there was a process involved. I couldn't simply respond with a letter and I had to wait for a hearing date. A week or two later the lawsuit was amended and everyone was dismissed from the case and fired from their jobs, along with several others. The only remaining defendants on the case were now me and Mark. Something was terribly wrong, I could sense something was off and that something was being coordinated. I hadn't been given an opportunity to respond and over a year had passed before I was able to give a deposition but by that time, life had turned upside down and my resolve to defend myself had completely eroded.

During the chaos of moving and being served a lawsuit, Susan emailed me to say that she had my personal laptop and wanted money from me to get it back. I had been looking for it and I asked my attorney to set up the exchange of her extorting money from me so that we had a paper trail. She spoke with him and he processed the exchange but she cashed my check and didn't return my personal property. I had to cut my losses while I had bigger concerns going with the lawsuit.

Aside from the worry of the lawsuit, Mark and I were getting along pretty well. I was hoping to get through this worrisome time together and I was feeling attached to him and wanted him to stay. I was relieved that he had quickly found a job; he started working directly for the owner of an IT company who had gotten him hired at Zantaz before Autonomy took over. The lawsuit consumed my life and my anxiety was at an all-time high as I worried every day about the outcome of this lawsuit. I wanted to have a response filed but I had to wait until a hearing date and I was hoping that would come soon. The ordeal was frightening and now we had this huge life event in common and we leaned on each other for support. No one else that I knew besides Mark could understand what I was going through. I'd been undergoing so much stress every waking moment and I wasn't feeling like myself. I was irritable and felt extremely tired all of the time and I had major headaches; but when I started feeling nauseous and I took a home pregnancy test and found that I was pregnant. Finally, some great news in all of the chaos of my life! I was very scared about how the future would play out but I was also excited and really looking forward to this new and happy beginning. I immediately made a doctor's appointment that was scheduled for a few weeks away but I wanted to wait until after my appointment to share the happy news with my side of the family. Mark couldn't contain his excitement and called his Mom to tell her the good news. I was anxious to see my doctor and while I waited for that day, I daydreamed about what motherhood was going to be like and stayed busy looking at baby clothes online and picking out names while he was at work.

17

SLEEPING WITH THE ENEMY

Rent came due but Mark hadn't given me any money and I asked him about it. "KJ is going to pay me in cash in a few days and its fine; you don't have nothing to worry about. He's got a bunch of contracts lined up now that his business is starting to take off." He went on to say that KJ and Don were working together to deliver and install hardware at various sites. My mouth went dry and my heart began to amplify loudly in my ears. "What? KJ and Don are in business now?" I asked. Mark abruptly stopped speaking and stared at me like a deer caught in headlights. "Mark, why are you working with Don? What are you doing?" I asked. He continued looking at me with a blank stare and quickly diverted his eyes. In that moment I knew he was lying to me about so many things. "What have you done?" I asked. "I haven't done anything. I told you I had to quit when they started asking me a bunch of questions at that meeting," he said. I hadn't known that he'd quit his job, he'd said he'd been fired. I'd caught him in another lie. "Are all of the guys from the filing now working with KJ and Don?" I asked. He nodded yes. "Well, some of them," he said. "Are you fucking crazy?!

What have you fucking done?" I screamed. When the charges against the entire list of original defendants had been dropped Mark said the men had cut a deal. They accepted being fired from their jobs in exchange for being removed from the lawsuit without further consequence which made no sense to me. No one had contacted me about cutting a deal; I hadn't yet had a chance to speak against what I had been accused of. I didn't know until that moment that Mark had lied to me and that he had quit his job and hadn't been fired. He didn't intend to tell me that they were all continuing to work together but he had slipped. They had all done something and he was covering it up for them and they were taking me along for the ride. "You've been lying to me. You threw me under the bus!" I picked up a drinking glass from the kitchen table and threw it at his head. He ducked and it shattered against the front door. "I don't know what the fuck you got caught doing, but you and all of those fucks have now trapped me into this!" I yelled. "This isn't about those fucking phones, is it? You fucking asshole! Look at what you have done! Look at what you have done to me…and to us!" I screamed as I held my stomach. "Get out! Get the fuck out! I hate you! Get out of my fucking life!" I shouted as loudly as I could. I was crying uncontrollably and the room was spinning; I needed to lie down. Mark and the others had used me as a scapegoat and I had played right into it. I was newly pregnant and I was trapped in their web of lies that were changing the trajectory of my life. I would be under his control for the rest of my life now that I was pregnant and suddenly my happy news felt like a fucking prison sentence.

Mark wouldn't leave and a few days later one of the women that had helped me move needed the favor returned but I didn't have the physical stamina and I was an emotional wreck. That morning I stayed home while Mark went to Amber's to lend a hand and he stayed helping her late into the evening because he'd said her friend that had planned to help her didn't show up. It was past ten when he came in and I didn't like that he had prioritized and played hero to an acquaintance of mine who was more like a stranger to me, while he had put me in a wake of destruction and was pretending to be the ever charming and happy helper. When he walked in I told him to get out and we got into an explosive argument and I hurled a plate at him and he left. He came back the following afternoon and he didn't say anything to me when he came in; I thought he'd stayed the night in his car and came in to get his clothes but he wasn't pulling them together and was in the kitchen getting something to eat. I asked him where he'd been and he said that he went back to Amber's to spend the night. I felt a piercing sting in my chest; he didn't care at all about what he was doing. He had played a victim to get me to feel badly for him so that'd I'd allow him to stay with me and he was ruining my life and he still had an appetite to eat. I felt disgusted and further betrayed. I wanted him out and gone from my home immediately but he continued to refuse to go. He said he had every right to be there now that he was on my lease. What the fuck was happening? I felt like I was on a runaway train and I was helpless to stop it. Before I could make sense of one major catastrophe, he was putting me in another and I felt disoriented. There was no end in sight - he didn't care about me or the pregnancy. I had been sleeping with the enemy all along and hadn't known. I felt trapped and I had almost the whole year remaining before my lease came due and by then the baby would be born. Fuck, how was I going to get us through this? I called my landlord to explain I wanted him out but he said I would lose my deposit and pay fees if I broke my lease. He was of no help to me and just wanted money and I couldn't afford to leave and I didn't have the money to move. I felt stuck in my own home. Graham was right, Mark was a miserable deadbeat. Worse, he had swindled me into playing a part in his scam and had used my belief in him and my kindness to take advantage of me.

Mark said he was going away for work with KJ and Don and my doctor's appointment came due. The happiness I felt at seeing the positive result on the home pregnancy test was a distant memory now. I couldn't find my bearings. I felt unable to see a way out of the predicament I was in and while in despair I made a heart wrenching decision to have an abortion. On the day of my abortion Mark was back and he came with me but I couldn't go through with it and I walked out of the appointment. I didn't want to make a harrowing decision while grief stricken but I didn't have much time to ponder the future. Fuck. I couldn't think straight. I couldn't change what he and the others were putting me through and the future looked bleak. I was so distraught but I rescheduled the appointment and I went without him.

We stayed living a miserable existence together and the lawsuit continued to drag on while I still hadn't had a chance to respond. I was so unhappy and when I would visit with friends I started drinking heavily on the days or evenings that we got together to escape from the horrors of my life. I used to be the life of the party and while having fun I was zany and funny when I'd have too much to drink, but now when I was with friends I was always the woman that was drowning out her sorrows. I was depressing to be around. I had tried so hard to get my life back on track when I had started working at my new job and had then met and moved in with Susan. Now, my life was a mess again. It was more than a mess, it was nightmare.

As the months passed by our deposition date was rescheduled several times; each time it would draw near it would be abruptly cancelled at the last moment and pushed out again. I was dealing with high anxiety at all times and I could barely eat or sleep from the worry of what was going to happen to me. I started thinking that it would be better if I was no longer alive and contemplated suicide. I couldn't face what was happening especially because I had no control over it. Mark had started an affair with a neighbor and I knew what was going on. I wasn't sleeping with him anymore and I was constantly screaming at him and throwing my dishes around in a fit of anger. I hated him for what he had done to me and if he wouldn't leave he had to witness how miserable I had become. I noticed he continued checking the mail every day at a very specific time and one day I went outside to see why he was always at the mailbox and saw him flirting with a red headed woman that lived a few doors away in another building. The closeness of their body language showed they were very comfortable with each other. When he came in I asked him about it and he said didn't know what I was talking about and that there wasn't a neighbor at all that he'd ever spoke to aside from saying hello to the man that lived next door. I knew he was lying because I had seen him. I later found a pornographic video clip of her downloaded on my new computer hard drive and he still denied they were having an affair.

I was becoming severely depressed and sleeping a lot more. Every time I looked in the mirror another piece of me had chipped away. I wanted him out and he still refused; he wouldn't go. One morning after he left for work I placed all of his belongings into his laundry basket outside of the front door. He had a key but I didn't want to let him back in and when he tried to open the door when he came back from work, I kept locking it. He hopped over the balcony fence and kicked on the slider trying to break it in. I called the police and he left but when they arrived they said there wasn't anything they could do. He came back and he wouldn't leave so I went to stay with my parents for a few days that lived two hours away. After I had left, I had to commute back each day and pass through town because I was enrolled in vocational training for Aesthetics. Mark didn't know that I had been stopping by each day and I could see that his car was parked each time I stopped by during the morning and then after classes, and so was the neighbors' car - the woman that he was having an affair with. I told my parents what had been going on and that I didn't go want to go home. My parents didn't believe me; they thought my anxieties were unfounded and that I was creating problems for myself. But they didn't know the full story of what Mark had done and what he was putting me through. I had already told dad this had to do with my helping Mark sell a few of his phones but as things had unfolded it became very clear Mark was lying about something when he started working with his old crew. I didn't want to tell them anything else and burden them with my problems. What was going on consumed me every waking moment of each day but I felt humiliated and angry for being duped and I didn't talk to them in detail about it because I still didn't know all of the details myself. As far as they knew, Mark was considered a new boyfriend and they hadn't known him long. They didn't know anything about him or that I had been seeing him on occasion for two years and that after he'd moved in that I had become pregnant and had an abortion. When I had told my dad that Mark was having affairs my dad looked at my quizzically and shook his head and said, "No, I don't think so." They had believed Mark's nice guy routine as did I and I couldn't tell them everything that was going on because it was all so convoluted. I was disheartened but I went home and Mark and I continued to stay in separate rooms. No matter how many times I asked him to leave, he wouldn't go. He wore me down and I was emotionally depleted. I could barely hang on to my sanity given everything that I was dealing with in a short span of time.

We had only a few months left on the lease and I had received an email one evening from a woman that said she was sleeping with Mark. When I confronted him about it he continued to deny having an affair with anyone and looked at me with a serious face and concern in his tone and said that I he didn't know why I continued to make up stories about affairs but that I was truly not well. Later that night we continued arguing and it escalated into another heated screaming match just as I was getting ready for bed. Mark jumped on me in my bed and flipped me over and held me down while he punched me in the back of my head repeatedly until I stopped struggling. Afterward he grabbed my new computer and snapped the screen off and threw it, putting a hole into the wall. I grabbed the heavy crystal lamp from my side table to hit him back but it stayed plugged into the wall and it fell out of grasp when I swung at him. I ran into the bathroom and called the police. The policeman arrived within minutes and was at first reluctant to arrest him because he could only see a scratch on my face. I had large bumps forming where he'd hit me on my head and the officer inspected me very closely with his flashlight through my hair as though he didn't believe me. He saw them then he arrested him. When Mark got outside he put on a dramatic show for the neighbors to look like an innocent and he turned around and shouted out to me as though he were being falsely arrested. He spent a week in jail and I hadn't been informed at the time to file a protection order and I didn't know that I could so I didn't. The following day after he beat me I went to a doctor that could see I was in a lot of pain in both my neck and head and he diagnosed me with whiplash and sent me home with a neck brace that I had to wear for several weeks. A few weeks later I received a barrage of harassing emails from the woman said that she was sleeping with Mark. She'd said that I was stupid for not seeing what was going on and went on to say that I should kill myself – while taunting me with knowledge of past traumas with the intention to bully me into suicide. The emails wouldn't stop coming in and it affected my work. I had the anonymous emails traced and found they were coming from Susan. I remembered that she had told me more than once how she enjoyed bullying the receptionist at her job for nothing more than sheer pleasure of watching how she hurt this woman. She was obsessed with me. She was still living with Bill but he was gone all day at work and it was obvious Mark was seeing her and that she was somehow involved in this lawsuit. Mark denied having an affair and when I told him that I knew that the emails were coming from Susan he immediately went silent mid-sentence. I knew he had been lying by his behavior and given what she'd said and what she was doing, it was obvious that Susan was one of his mistresses. Mark had pulled me into his mess and there were no limits to his betrayal.

18

ALTERNATE REALITY

I had been put through so much within a matter of months that I officially came undone. I had a nervous breakdown within days of my last conversation with Mark about the emails from Susan and I went to see a psychiatrist. Inside of thirty minutes he diagnosed me with bipolar disorder and prescribed a powerful cocktail of medications that he started me on from the trial packs that he had in his office. He didn't have all of the facts within our first appointment or knew of the events that had transpired that caused the extreme stress; we only talked about my present state of mind. But I took the pills and trusted that it was for the best; I didn't know they would be addictive and that they would alter my personality and physicality but they numbed me from reality very quickly and I wanted so desperately to escape what was happening because the alternative was suicide. Very soon after taking them I could barely function and nothing bothered me – I wasn't sad anymore, angry or frightened. I wasn't happy either and I couldn't laugh anymore, I couldn't find joy in the simple pleasures of life. But I liked it because absolutely nothing mattered anymore and I was no longer thinking of suicide. Life passed and I was functioning but it felt like I stayed staring at a grey wall all day only to see it turn black when I closed my eyes at night. With my cognitive functioning and my senses highly dimmed, I simply existed and my emotions were removed. The pills behaved like a modern day lobotomy. I had a terrible time concentrating in my classes and I became very withdrawn from friends that I'd known and regularly spoke with for years. My business and work as an artist was now further affected by the meds. I began forgetting basic makeup techniques that I had done hundreds of times and I could hardly hold my brushes. I developed severe cramping in my hands and they shook involuntarily as though I had Parkinson's disease. I also gained eighty pounds over the next few months, it was debilitating. I also developed a host of other embarrassing physical ailments that were created from the side-effects; I no longer looked like myself and was practically stuck in the bathroom all of the time because I couldn't eat anything without having to use the restroom. I could see in the mirror each morning that the light in my eyes shifted to darkness as I moved along in an alternate reality and I didn't want to look at myself anymore so I kept my head down and my eyes closed when I had to brush my teeth and wash my hands at the bathroom sink. My wardrobe sat unworn and collected dust as I continued to grow out of my clothes; I could only fit into stretch pants and stretch tops.

The lease was coming due and Mark was no longer solely working with KJ, Don and the others because they had put him to work but weren't paying him. He found employment at Robert Half Int'l., and I no longer cared that Mark was living with me or what he had done or was doing because I couldn't feel my emotions anymore. Nothing bothered me. He enjoyed how different and subdued I was and would often bring me my pills before I went to sleep at night. He talked often of how much better he liked me now that I was on medication because he could have his way with me. At first I thought he'd said it as a joke but he continued to always say this throughout our relationship. He was with me all of the time now everywhere I went and he would often tell my friends and parents how much I had changed for the better now that I was on medication and nothing bothered me. They assumed he was referring to the meds having quelled my overwhelming angst and anxieties but I knew that wasn't what he meant and over time I didn't think about it anymore. I used to speak up, stand up for myself and react in anger to his mistreatment and now nothing at all disturbed me in the least. We started having sex again every day but now it was several hours long. The euphoria I felt during climax was the only bliss I could feel in my life and I became addicted to the release of the hormones that coursed through my body. It kept me tethered and connected to him after my world came undone and I went into an alternate reality; he was a sex addict and I was never short of his supply.

The end of my lease had finally arrived, I used to count down the days but now I waited a few more months after it expired before putting in notice. I was no longer angry but I made plans to stay with my parents for a short time. Mark did nothing to find another place to live when I said that I was moving out and I continued to remind him but on our final night in my condo, Mark came in after work to see my things had been removed and was surprised. The place was empty except for the blanket and pillow I was sleeping with until the morning. He lay down beside me and pulled me close to have sex and afterward he spooned me and I heard him sniffling and I felt his body begin to shake and he started sobbing as he buried his face in my hair. I had every reason to walk away and to stop caring about him, but I did care. Even though he had hurt me and took advantage of me in so many ways I felt bad for him again. He didn't have anywhere to go and I felt awful. I turned around and hugged him back and he buried his face in the crook of my neck and he cried himself to sleep. I'd never seen him cry like that and I didn't know what to make of it; it was as if he was crying like a little boy. He seemed so pitiful and sorrowful that I doubted I was making the right decision by moving on. We parted ways in the morning and Mark called me after two days and said he was sleeping in a hotel. I felt terrible for leaving him in such distress and I offered to help him look for a new place and he rented a studio apartment not far from his job. He and I continued to see each other again, one to three times a week, and it stayed like this throughout the duration of the case and for a year after the lawsuit had closed.

19

COERCION

A few months after I moved out we were scheduled to appear for our deposition hearing. I didn't have the determination or the focus I'd had at the start but I still wanted to answer their questions and respond in my own words to the accusations. Autonomy said they needed more time to compile discovery files and that was why the hearing date continually moved out. It felt as though I were on trial. When I met with my attorney on strategy I pushed back on the approach that I should remain silent upon questioning. Mark's attorney was taking that stance and I knew that because Mark had told me. After his and my attorney spoke, it was decided this was the best strategy and I didn't want to do it because I knew the men were conspiring together after Mark had moved in to my place and started working with them. However, my attorney informed me that my case was about different hardware and this filing was much larger than a few cell phones that Mark had sold; it was about embezzlement and fraud and the sale of high-ticket hardware items. With his urging and advice, I relented. On the day of my deposition their team of attorney's lined up in single file fashion and paraded around the table carrying several filing boxes. If those were the discovery files they were collecting all this time, I hadn't been given a copy of them, I thought. At any rate, I didn't have the capacity to read through that many documents and had left that up to my attorney. It was a very frightening and intimidating process and it had taken over a year for me to have my chance to respond to this lawsuit filing and yet so much had happened in that time. Autonomy had half dozen lawyers that worked the case and they continued to drag this out for as long as they needed to. I knew they didn't have anything on me but my resolve had eroded and I felt incapable of speaking up or standing up for myself any longer. However, I had relented and as agreed, I took the advice of my attorney and plead the fifth for every question that was asked during my deposition. I had tried to speak up to one of the questions when they slid a piece of paper across to me that showed my email address with a query to Mark about phones. I looked at my attorney with confusion because I hadn't sent anything and wanted to speak but he got very angry and slammed his pen down and I quickly shut down. My silence would later be taken as an admission of guilt and as some misaligned loyalty to Mark – because I had no testimony to provide. In other words I had no evidence to submit to prove my innocence to the false accusations.

For nearly another year Autonomy scheduled and rescheduled the final hearing to submit plaintiff testimony. I stayed in a state of high anxiety; as each date would draw near, the hearing would be cancelled and reschedule for another month away. They had done this since the start of the filing and I wanted this rollercoaster to end, I'd even told my attorney that I'd be willing to admit to anything and go to prison right then if it meant it would end. Very suddenly a new date was made and we were asked to be there within a week. We were there to hear plaintiff testimony and then hear the ruling. On that day Mark and I drove in together because his car had recently gotten repossessed and he asked me

WHAT'S IN EMERALD CITY?

if I could pick him up along the way, I was driving from my parents' home. I could barely drive anymore and could only drive in town and never at night; I had developed agoraphobia and had difficulty driving the freeways, I could drive them but I would have a panic attack. My attorney was a 2.5 hours' drive from my parents' home and for some of those appointments my dad had to drive for me because there was so much fog that I couldn't leave. I didn't have the confidence to handle driving anymore, it was impossible now if there was inclement weather. I had been prescribed Xanax; this drug is highly addictive and is very sedating. It impairs cognitive functioning and makes you very tired and listless. It also makes you feel extremely hung-over, similar to having had way too much to drink and you feel very groggy the next morning and can barely move. You cannot come out of it and simply shake it off, especially if you are taking them regularly every day. My prescription was a powerful dose at 1mg per pill that was recommended up to 3 times a day and more as needed. If I had panic attacks I took 6mg in a day. On the day of plaintiff testimony I woke up in a tiresome haze from having taken 6mg of Xanax throughout the day before, and I had to use all of my strength to get out of bed. Fortunately it was sunny out and dad asked me a few times if he should drive because the hearing was near my attorney's office but I said I could it, I didn't want to tell him that I was picking up Mark. I left the house with several hours ahead of me so that I could navigate the winding country roads before getting on the freeway where I drove less than the speed limit in the slow lane. I was petrified but my senses were dulled while I drove the two hours to San Ramon and afterward Mark drove us the remaining half hour to San Francisco. Mark had said that we were probably going to be listening to testimony from someone that he'd spoken with the day he had quit his job. We got to the building and parked and as we came up the elevator and exited into the hallway to meet our attorney's, Susan was standing there. Mark avoided eye contact with her and walked into another room. At my deposition hearing nearly a year prior, the boxes of discovery I had seen were not evidence that had been presented at any point of any wrong doing on my part. They were empty file boxes for all I knew carried by a team of attorney's set to intimidate me so that I'd keep silent. My deposition hearing had long ago passed and I had already pleaded the fifth and therefore didn't have evidence to submit on my own behalf. We were there to listen to plaintiff testimony and afterward hear the ruling. Autonomy didn't have proof that I'd done anything wrong and they had repeatedly dragged this date out for several months but now Susan was there to take a seat. I wasn't given a chance to speak on anything that she'd said because my deposition was over. I was in a no-win situation from the very start of this lawsuit and they were manufacturing evidence as they went along. She read from a script of notes that I had watched her scribble down in the hallway on a small piece of paper. I sat there listening to her tell a fabricated story of lies and untruths. Mark had gotten arrested for stealing from his company two years prior and now the plaintiff testimony was mostly about me. It was extremely testing to sit there and watch her lie while I knew I didn't have a chance to reply and if not for the sedation I would have jumped over the table and punched her. She gave a contradictory statement at the start when she said she had knowledge of activities and gave dates in 2008 which aligned with when she was in jail. Further I had not worked at Autonomy, Mark worked for Autonomy. I had stopped working under Zantaz in May 2007 when Autonomy bought the company. She was their sole witness and it was obvious to me that she was scheming with the plaintiff as they led her with their questions and she read her scrawled cliff notes in response from a torn piece of scratch paper. The arbitrator simply sat and listened and then asked only one question. Why she was coming forward and doing all of this? Susan went on to say that it needed to stop and that she felt badly for me for what I was involved in. Everything Susan said was a web of lies. Aside from her affair with Mark, Susan had other motivating factors to be there. She hated that my life was carefree and while I lived in her condo I was working hard at my new business during a crashing economy and going to school, as she had been jailed for DUI/DV and had a baby while incarcerated, and was then forced to stay shackled at home on house arrest with a man she despised for putting her there. I was watching a circus show. My attorney told the arbitrator that she was there because she was jealous. Without the arbitrator understanding the entire backstory of who Susan was and how I knew her she didn't understand or see that Susan wanted to take from me and wanted to swap places so that I would live her miserable existence. We weren't there to provide additional testimony, only there to hear what the plaintiff had to say. Also, Mark had sold her two used cell phones and delivered them to her at Bill's. She had Mark arrested for her own reasons and subsequently asked me to move out. She was a lying criminal who extorted money from me, harassed and bullied me, caused me severe mental distress and according to the emails I traced back to her had admitted to sleeping with Mark. I could see that she was working with the plaintiff and I could see that she had an agenda and that she had gone out of her way to do these things. She had several reasons that motivated her to be there. A week prior to our final arbitration hearing she called my attorney in an effort to threaten and intimidate us and when he answered his phone, she identified herself and went on an incoherent and rambling tirade while screaming obscenities at him. Susan's testimony had been orchestrated from the start and the arbitrator ate it up. We had been there for about half an hour while we sat listening to her lies and we broke for lunch; my attorney said he was starving and he quickly left so that he could eat. I sat there waiting for the lunch hour to pass and when we resumed I listened to a few last words from one of the internal corporate attorney's that was employed at Autonomy as he spoke about Mark's activities. Afterward the arbitrator settled in favor of the plaintiff and I was found guilty of fraud alongside Mark.

Sure, I had helped Mark place a few ads and sell some of his phones when he'd asked me to. I was more than willing to speak on that before my deposition but when this lawsuit dragged on it became evident that it wasn't about the phones, it had to do with high-ticket hardware items. I didn't have anything to do with an inside job with high ticket hardware items for the IT industry. I had been hoodwinked into being forced to remain silent in my defense and then later didn't have a chance to speak up against the web of lies that Susan told. Mark took his charade as far as he could go all the while proclaiming his innocence but I knew the truth when I'd found out he was continuing to work with Don and the others after he'd quit Autonomy and after he had moved in with me. I knew I had been setup. I was now branded a thief and criminal, and pointed to as a mastermind in some elaborate inside scheme for a company I had never worked for. Autonomy was using the Zantaz name to charge me because they now owned the name and that's how they tied me in to lay blame. I was held half liable for a $1M restitution settlement awarded to the plaintiff plus hundreds of thousands in additional attorney's fees. My life, reputation and my name was dismantled and ruined. I'd once had a twelve year career working at various companies as an Executive Assistant and I worked incredibly hard since I was a teenager and had made very good money as a young woman without degree. Susan had known that when she had taken my unemployment filing to fax in without my permission, she had seen that I had made twice as much money as she did. I would never find another employer to hire me again if I ever needed to go back to working for someone else. Autonomy said that if I did, they would garnish my wages and fight me in court against a bankruptcy filing. Meanwhile Susan, who had perjured herself and colluded with Autonomy, went free of any charges and so did the ring of men that had defrauded the company from the inside.

The settlement was awarded. There was a petition hearing a few months later on October 28, 2011 to confirm the arbitration award for the plaintiff but I was advised that the appeals process was not something easily overturned and that lack of funds prevented me from continuing with counsel. In that same month Autonomy sold their company to Hewlett Packard for $11.7 billion dollars.

20

THE TABLES HAVE TURNED

A year after HP purchased Autonomy they wrote off $8.8 billion of Autonomy's value and cited major culture clashes between the companies in the press[5]. HP claimed the clashes resulted from "accounting improprieties, misrepresentations, and disclosure failures" by previous management[6]. The lawsuit that HP filed claimed that during 2009 to 2011 (the same years of my case), Autonomy purchased a few companies and embarked on an internal scheme to defraud them by inflating the value of their company and claiming their high profit margins were due to their software-only product but were secretly reselling hardware equipment on the side[7]. And, that Autonomy was creating exaggerated performance claims by manipulating financial data in their accounting practices in an effort to inflate the value of their company to shareholder and stakeholders. It was discovered that in 2009 an internal whistle blower at Autonomy raised concerns about the accounting practices and many people were paid off, intimidated into silence and threatened, while others were scapegoated to take a fall so that their internal fraud system continued. To get the heat off from what the employee uncovered, the company placed the focus elsewhere and used me as one of those scapegoats.

Autonomy used my employment with Zantaz to tie me to a lawsuit. When I had been hired on at Zantaz in 2006, I signed a standard new-hire HR form that dictated any court proceedings would be held in arbitration – a private hearing that would not go public with a judge and jury trial. I was laid off in May 2007 after Autonomy purchased Zantaz, and Autonomy now owned the name[4]. When Susan called in to complain about Mark's activities it created a ripple effect. Autonomy's scheme was about to be uncovered when an internal employee in the early part of 2009 had looked into the accounting department and saw they were cooking the books. Autonomy came up with a ruse and they needed to blame shift to cover up the corruption that had been discovered in 2009 so they could continue their scheme through 2011. Unbeknownst to me at the time, Mark had been a guilty party to the conspiracy but he had quit when he had gotten questioned, he wasn't fired, and therefore was pinned as the fall guy. He had originally signed on with the company as a crossover from Zantaz and had also signed the same standard HR arbitration form that I had. It didn't seem plausible that a low-level IT tech could have possibly carried out such an elaborate scheme on his own, but they knew he was dating me, the former executive assistant that had previously worked under Zantaz. Autonomy paid out several people to keep their scheme going because there were billions of dollars at stake if they were found out and a jury trial went public. They had plans to sell their company and they colluded with Susan and fed her a testimony that she would give so that it would look concrete that I had been involved alongside with Mark in his fraud activities. Was she paid off? It's plausible because they had the money to do it and they paid off several people. The arbitrator was never going to hear a response from me or find out that Susan was a former roommate/landlord and that she had a criminal background and a history of obsessive and harassing behavior toward me, that she herself had bought phones from Mark, that she was on house arrest and couldn't leave her home or that she carried on an affair with him. It wasn't going to be discovered that the dates she provided when calling into Mark's employer aligned with when she was in jail. None of that mattered anyway, because I had been pressured and intimidated into pleading the fifth long before plaintiff testimony and therefore had no evidence that was submitted to prove my innocence. Additionally, I didn't get along with the employees that were listed on the original lawsuit filing in 2009 when I had worked with them in 2007 at Zantaz, and they all knew that Mark and I were seeing each other because he had told them when we started dating. Once Autonomy decided on their plan of action, these employees were then let go and subsequently dismissed from the arbitration case. Afterward, these individuals and Mark continued to work together fulfilling deliveries and installations of high-ticket hardware purchases under a third party contracting company that worked with Autonomy. The owner of this contracting company was someone Mark knew personally and had helped him get hired on at Zantaz. Autonomy continued their fraud throughout the duration of my lawsuit from 2009-2011 and as it turned out - it had all been orchestrated by those at the very top[8].

After many years of litigation HP won a successful fraud case that was brought against Autonomy CFO Sushovan Hussein, he was convicted of fraud and sentenced to 5 years in prison in May 2019 and began serving his sentence during the COVID-19 Pandemic in August 2020[9]. HP is currently pursuing a civil lawsuit against Autonomy founder, Mike Lynch, for overseeing $5B in fraud dating from 2009 to 2011. To date, he is fighting extradition charges to the US and HP is awaiting a verdict on their filing in the UK[10] (update January 28, 2022,

HP wins fraud case in the UK against Mike Lynch[11]). The others that colluded with the company to defraud the buyers and had worked to dismantle my life in the process haven't been charged.

21

THE MASK

At the end of the case, we separated. I had two pets that I shuttled around with me between when I stayed at Mark's place and with my parents. Soon after we separated they suddenly died within days of each other and I was beside myself with grief. Mark was continuing to call and I leaned on him for support and I went back to him. Everything felt like it continued to fall apart and we ended up staying attached to each other for another year after the case. It was as though I had an invisible chain around my neck that tethered me to him. I was still taking heavy medication and my doctor had increased my dosages, I felt listless and utterly hopeless of positive change – I couldn't think straight. Outwardly it appeared I was making conscious decisions but I wasn't myself in the least and my life, personality and behavior had drastically altered. If not for the pills things would have been handled much differently in every area of my life. It was hard to reconcile what I had gone through over the years and now I had lost my beloved pets. I was but a mere fragment and a shell of my former self and I purposefully stayed consciously sedated to get through a life that was hard to face. The pills had overrun me but I couldn't stop taking them if I'd wanted to. I had developed a dependency on them because the ingredients were extremely addictive and caused a lot of anguish if I tried to stop them. If I ceased taking them, I couldn't go past 24 hours without severe withdrawals and was told I could have seizures that could lead to death. The pills continued to keep me from feeling and working through my emotions and I didn't want to face my grim reality – they kept me checked out. Over time there were more red flags to Mark's affairs and women were starting to come to his apartment but my senses were so dimmed down, I was extremely vulnerable and very easy to manipulate. There were many times I had an inclination to the truth but I can't overly stress how the medication dulled my senses and robbed me of my faculties and capability to defend myself against many things or see the large red flags of a painful reality. I didn't have any friends that ever pulled me to the side and had an honest conversation over how I'd changed or wanted to know if I were ok; instead, I was the topic for discussion and gossip when I left the table. No one came to my defense but instead contributed to taking advantage of me in various ways, my kindness taken as a weakness and I constantly over did at the asking like a puppet where as I was not like that before. These so-called friends and family members had been in secret competition with me all along and enjoyed watching my fall while pretending to care.

It didn't take much for Mark to know how to continue his manipulation tactics and he had a ready answer for anything. While these other women in his life, even some of my own friends and family, played along with him, I was manipulated so I wouldn't know or be suspicious. Because of my sedation, it wasn't difficult for things to slip past me very easily. However Mark also didn't want me to leave him because of the benefits I provided to his life so he continued to lie to me about sleeping with other women and in some cases, men, to keep me in his life and prevent me from finding happiness with someone who truly could value and love me. While I was in a fog I had grown accustomed to ignoring my intuition and accepted his behavior – forgetting the past mistakes and how he'd treated me I began to see him as a truthful person that had the worst luck in life. It's laughable to draw that conclusion when I look back on it now and it makes me very sad at how I had been taken advantage of by so many monstrous people. Mark had most of the week to easily live a double life and I barely had energy to argue about anything anymore; we bickered at times but we didn't have the drawn out arguments that we once did while he once lived with me. I'd given up on myself and let myself go while I stayed in the haze created by the meds. That worked very well for me because I continued to escape from life and it worked even better for Mark as he continued to benefit from my adaptability and remained malleable to his whims.

Mark had gone into debt and was walking to work because his car had been repossessed. I helped him buy a new bike and loaned him my car for stretches of time. One morning during the week, he got up as usual he had showered and then leaned to kiss me goodbye and left for work. He was walking that day and it was early and still dark outside before he walked out. About an hour later Mark charged into the studio and kicked the door in and it flew open. Confused and very groggy from the medication I didn't know what was happening but I was jolted from my sleep and opened my eyes as I lay there. "Wake up, wake up!" he yelled. "What's going on? What's the matter?" I asked. "I just saw someone getting raped!" he yelled. Mark looked wild eyed. "What? What are you talking about?" I asked sleepily. I was slowly sitting up now and trying my best to wipe the sleep from my eyes. The pills made it so hard to wake up, I was exhausted but he'd frightened me when he barged into the studio and I was awake. "Wait, slow down. Did you call the police? Where did this happen?" I asked. "Right at my job. I was walking up behind the building and there was this guy on top of a girl having sex. When I got up close I could hear the girl saying 'no' and 'stop' and she didn't seem to be all there," he said. "What do you mean, 'not all there'?" I asked. "Yeah. She wasn't all there. She was drugged or drunk and she tried to push him off. So I walked up behind him and stomped him like this" he said as he gestured with his leg. "I kept him down and called the cops then left a statement when they got there. I went into work and told my supervisor what happened and she said I was a hero and gave me the day off." I laid there listening and then he turned to walk toward the bathroom. "That's crazy. Why didn't you call me to pick you up? How did you get home?" I said. "I was scared and ran all the way here," he said. "Scared of what?" I asked. "You didn't see what I saw! That was scary seeing that!" Mark said. He was breathing hard and had a wild look in his eyes. "I'm gonna take another shower." He walked into the bathroom, closing the door behind him. I didn't know what to think as I lay there replaying the events over the recent couple of weeks in my mind, but I was very uneasy.

Mark had recently purchased a Taser gun, ski mask and gloves and was leaving his apartment in the mornings wearing them with the Taser in his jacket. I had asked him several times why he had them and he said it was for protection and that his face was freezing in the cold mornings while he walked or rode his bike to work. I wasn't convinced because I knew Mark had worked as a bouncer and security guard at previous jobs long before we met and that he had karate training. He was also tall and naturally muscular. There was a series of irrational behavior and events that had unfolded that led up to him showing me he had the Taser.

I had been loaning him my car but had taken it back after I'd seen he put thousands of miles on it within a month's time. During this same time my ex-boyfriend JD had contacted me online and Mark had intercepted his messages. I had received alerts on my phone and when I checked my account I saw that Mark was angrily corresponding with him and telling him that he was my boyfriend. When I confronted Mark he said that he knew accessing my account was wrong but that he had the passwords to everything I had since we'd started dating because I'd given them to him. I had no idea until then that he had access to my email and social accounts and that I was being monitored the entire time that we were dating. I had not given Mark permission or access to any of my email or social accounts but he continued to insist that I had and then got angry with me because JD had reached out to me. A few nights later Mark and I went to see a movie and after we parked my car and walked to the entrance, he said he'd left his wallet behind and went back for it. I went inside to wait in line for our food so that Mark could come back in and pay for the movie tickets and meet me in the food court. Mark was wearing a t-shirt he'd bought at Target that said 'Military' across the chest and I quickly spotted him when he came back into the corridor. As he stood in line to pay for our tickets he was speaking to an elderly couple in front of him and I could see that he was all smiles and laughing and being very animated. When Mark walked over to me I asked him what the conversation was about but the elderly man approached us and cheerily shook Mark's hand while his wife smiled on. He told Mark thank you for his service and that he was honored to meet him and that the least he could do was buy a ticket for a fellow man that served his country to protect us. "What?" I asked as I looked at Mark in horror. "This good man was generous enough to buy me a ticket, sweetheart." "Good man, sir, good man, thank you thank you. Enjoy your movie folks and thanks again. Have a good night!" Mark said to the couple with a big and charming smile. They said goodbye to us and added that I must be so proud and happy to have him back home and then walked on. I was mortified that he'd impersonated being a military vet to con an elderly couple out of a movie ticket. I was angry with him and we sat in the theater in uncomfortable silence waiting for the movie to start and afterward during low moments of silence during our movie he would say embarrassing remarks to humiliate me. While I ignored him he continued. He didn't care what he'd done to the elderly couple and was irritated with me for ruining his night. When we came out of the theater I noticed when I got into the passenger side that my car door was unlocked and saw that the keys were in the ignition. He had left my car running and he'd done it on purpose. We rarely argued anymore but I'd had enough and we got into a huge argument over the elderly couple and my car as we drove out of the parking lot and as we entered the freeway he punched me twice in the face with his left fist. I felt a crunching sensation in my jaw and it popped as my head hit the window. I was caught by surprise and put my hand on my face where he'd hit me and I just looked at him. He punched me again in the mouth and my head hit the side window again and I bit my tongue and felt a piece of my tooth in my mouth. I thought he'd split my lip at first because there was blood and I burst into tears and told him to stop hitting me and he told me to shut the fuck up or that he'd hit me again and he raised his fist. I stared out of the window and softly cried. He knew I was incapable of leaving and driving off when we got to his place. I was in a constant state of extreme anxiety when I wasn't sleeping and had developed agoraphobia after I started taking my medications and it hindered my driving. I could barely drive on the freeway during the day time, I avoided it at all costs and I could no longer drive at all at night. When we got to his place I pushed him out of my way as I made my way to the bathroom and he punched me in the arm. I screamed out for him to stop hitting me and went into the bathroom to look at my face. The blood had been from biting my tongue and I looked to see where my tooth had chipped because it hadn't come from the front. The bruising was already forming on my face, fuck, I thought. He hit me so hard on my upper arm I could barely move it. I stayed in there for almost an hour and then I heard a buzzing sound coming from the room. I didn't know what it was so I came out and he was standing across the room looking at something in his hands and he looked up at me. I asked him what he was holding and he told me it was a Taser gun. He then added that he bought it for protection and then he turned it off. I asked him how it worked and he said that he had to touch someone with it and an electrical current would render them helpless. I didn't say anything more to him and got into bed. He brought me my pills and I took my medication and fell asleep. On the days that I was there Mark began leaving his studio apartment with the Taser gun and wearing his ski mask and gloves.

The day after Mark had seen the girl getting sexually assaulted near his work building, a private investigator from the D.A.'s office called his cell phone around the time he'd come back in from work. He wanted more details about what had happened and I heard Mark tell the P.I. he didn't have more to add besides what he'd already told the officer that took his statement and immediately hung up. He looked like he'd been kicked in the stomach. "What's the matter?" I asked. "That was a P.I. calling for the D.A.'s office. They said they wanted to know more but I don't have anything else to say" he said. "Well, what's wrong? Why do you look like that?" I asked. "The P.I. said he wanted me to know that the guy is her boyfriend and she's underage." "Oh my god! How old is she?" I asked. "I don't know." he said. "You look sick, are you ok?" I asked. "I'm not feeling good, I'm gonna lay down." he said while holding his stomach. Mark lay down and went to sleep. After that day he stopped wearing the ski mask altogether and gave it to his child to play with and he called him Spiderman. Several calls came in from the D.A.'s office over the next few weeks and Mark refused to answer them and sent them to voicemail. I asked him to play one of the messages and heard the P.I. asking for his help in their case; he wanted to ask him a few questions that could really help them he'd said, but Mark refused to return any of his calls.

Mark's behavior had been becoming increasingly more erratic and aggressive. He was convinced the world was coming to an end and papered his office parking lot and employee desks with photocopies of bible scriptures. He told me that he'd been asked by his HR department if he'd done it and had lied to them but they'd said someone had seen him and he was given a verbal warning. They asked if he needed to take a leave of absence but he refused. Meanwhile the P.I. continued to call for a long while to leave messages and eventually he had left a final message to say the girls' boyfriend had been found guilty of the rape charge. I asked him why he wouldn't call the P.I. back to help him but he said he didn't want to get involved further and that he had already told the officer that questioned him everything he knew. It didn't make sense because he told everyone about what had happened and that he was a hero but Mark never returned any of the P.I.'s calls.

22

GOODBYE NARK

A few weeks after the P.I. stopped calling I was at Mark's place one afternoon when soon after he'd come in from work there was a knock at the door. At first I thought that maybe it was the P.I. because Mark didn't receive visitors and I could see that he didn't want to answer the door. He looked uncomfortable that someone had knocked and I got up but he stopped me and looked through the peep hole. He seemed perplexed when he looked outside and I could see an older woman standing there through the blinds that were slightly opened at the window near the door. His studio was in a gated community and I assumed the woman was a neighbor but Mark didn't want to greet her. I asked him who was outside and he shrugged as if to say he didn't know but he looked like he was sick again and I knew something was wrong. The woman knocked again and I went to open the door and he blocked me out of the way and opened it just enough to poke his head outside. I heard this woman say hello as though she knew him and I pulled the door open from his grasp and I smiled and was met with a look of surprise as she stood there in silence and stared at him. I hadn't met her before and didn't know who she was; she looked like someone's grandmother. She was much older than us and had long wild, curly, salt and pepper hair. She had on eyeglasses and wasn't wearing makeup and was very plainly dressed. She was very unassuming and for a quick moment I thought she was a religious person going door to door because Mark didn't go to church but was always carrying his bible. I invited her inside and she looked very distressed and upset so and I asked her if she was ok as I sat down in a chair near the door. She stood just inside of the threshold and refused to look at me and Mark introduced her as his coworker, Laura. I'd heard all about her because she had bought him bed sheets. He said they were a random Christmas gift from a company party and that a coworker named Laura had purchased them as a white elephant gift. However they were the size of his bed and had a masculine pattern, it was such an intimate gift that I didn't believe him and to prove his point they sat unopened in the corner of his room for months. He had gone on about her being such a nice and sweet old lady and said that she'd offered to let him stay in her spare room in her home and that it was all his if he wanted it, including use of her car. That only heightened my suspicions but when I continued to press him if he were having an affair with her he denied it. He'd said they were work friends and frequently took lunch together and went on walks every day. That he'd confide in her and they would hug each other but nothing more. It all sounded very familiar and we'd gotten into several arguments over her; I told him he should take her offer and move in with her but he denied having an affair and he got very angry with me and yelled that he wasn't remotely interested in her like that. He pointed out that I was being insanely jealous over a coworker who was an old lady and that the suggestion and thought repulsed him and afterward we would have sex as he'd tell me he loved me. When I saw her I instantly believed him and felt awful for the disagreements that I'd caused. She stared up at him and glanced over at me nervously and then put her hand to her forehead and said she was having a terrible day at work and that she wanted to talk to him about it. Mark stared back at her blankly and didn't say anything. I asked her again if she wanted to sit down but she refused and said she was leaving and walked out. When his phone rang a few minutes later he didn't want to pick up so I'd asked who it was and he said it was her, so I told him to answer. I saw that he tried to adjust the volume on his phone while he placed it to his ear but he had mistakenly turned it to high and not low and I could hear her ask him if I was still there. He'd said yes and played along by asking if she was ok and if there was anything he could do, but she said no and they agreed to speak at work the following day. It didn't seem plausible by looking at her that they were carrying on but I knew Mark was a pathological liar and from his behavior and the conversation I heard on the phone I knew for certain he was lying about their affair. He had a pattern of meeting women at work and them for sex and their resources. Mark continued to deny and had a complete meltdown and got very angry again that I continued to suggest it. He had a ready answer for how she got into the gate and as always, I started to doubt that they had anything going on because of his display and how angry he had gotten. It wasn't on my mind again after he gave me my medication that night and I went to sleep. All of my emotions and upsets were erased after I took my pills.

A week later I was sleeping and an hour after Mark had left for work, he came bursting in and kicked his door open. "Wake up, wake up!" he yelled. I was startled awake; this was becoming a regular occurrence with him. He'd said that he'd just been in a fist fight and while on his way to work a man had jumped out of the bushes. "What? He just attacked you?" I asked sleepily. I could barely talk, I was so groggy. "Are you ok, did you get mugged?" I asked in disbelief. "No! I hit him and then Tased him and he went down on his back and I ran off." he said. "Did he just scare you and catch you by surprise? What exactly happened?" I asked. "He tried to come out the bushes and put hands on me! He was grabbing at my junk!" he said. "What? You need to call the police." I said in alarm. He continued on and said that after he ran off and was near his workplace, the man came chasing after him on a bike and that he'd pulled him off and began punching him and then Tased him again and again until he lost consciousness. Mark said he then ran to work and was given the day off and that he then ran home. He went to take another shower and when he came from the bathroom I asked more questions. I wanted to know why he didn't call the police or call me to pick him up from work if there was some random man on the loose that had assaulted him, but he said he didn't feel well and needed to lie down and take a nap.

A couple of weeks later on a Friday, he and I were outside and Laura drove into the parking lot. She stopped her car and gave him an angry scowl, she looked at him then at me and looked back at him and shook her head. She wagged her finger at him and then sped off. I didn't know what to think but it was strange. Mark got very angry and immediately dialed the police from his cell phone to report that someone he worked with kept driving by his home and that he was being stalked. The dispatcher had an officer call back and he told Mark that if she returned, to call them back and that they'd come to his apartment. He also strongly encouraged Mark to file a restraining order if he felt that she was a danger to him. Mark told him that she was and he later filed the paperwork and had Laura served the following week. A few days afterward he was fired from his job when she went to their HR department and said that he tried to grab at her shirt and attempted to assault her during their lunch time while they were having a discussion. On the day he was fired, he came in and rushed into the apartment again. He pushed the door in with such force and it woke me from my sleep and yelled that he had been fired. This time I didn't respond to anything he had to say. On the one hand it seemed Laura was being retaliatory but there were so many dramatic occurrences unfolding with such frequency that I could clearly see there was a repetitive pattern to his behavior. When I didn't respond, he just looked at me waiting for a reaction but when I didn't give one he went into the bathroom to shower. I laid there shaken that he had been fired for attempted assault and I didn't know if he was going to get arrested or what might unfold. He had filed the protection order but was awaiting his hearing date to go before the judge but things seemed to be taking a very ugly turn. When he came out of the bathroom he wanted to lie down and he closed his eyes and started talking about a time he had been accused of sexual assault at another job and had also been fired. I was alarmed and froze in fear but asked him to go on. He continued and said that he had once worked for the Oakland Unified School District and had been fired because a twelve year old girl had claimed he was her boyfriend and had told some of her friends at school that they were having sex. Mark went on to say that they had become friends outside of his work and I asked him why he would have that friendship with a twelve year old girl and he'd said he knew that it was wrong that he'd been to her house because she had a crush on him but that she reminded him of his days as a youth camp counselor and that he was visiting with her as though he was a 'big brother'. I remembered the stories about his counselor days very well because they revolved around sex between him and other consenting teens he'd said. I always assumed he was a youth as well but now I wasn't sure. He went on to say that his boss at the school district had quietly let him go but that he had been working for KJ and was a contractor at that job and that he then found him a placement for hire at Zantaz. Now I felt sick, something was very wrong and I didn't know why he was telling me all of this. I wasn't going to continue to stand by his side or be drawn into his predicament by becoming his shelter and fall guy again. He was unloading his catalog of deception. I had also recently helped him pay for a supplemental technical certification at his urging and had found he didn't have a technical degree. He said that he could make a lot more money if he'd had the certification but he didn't seem interested in completing the program. I had been asking him every day for the money and I wanted to know why he hadn't tackled the course work but he gave excuses and when I asked how far he had gotten he hadn't even started it. He reluctantly told me that he didn't know how to do it and admitted that he'd been getting his jobs in IT by using his twin brothers' college credentials on his applications. He explained that their names and social security numbers were very similar and that no one had questioned it and that he figured things out on the job. He'd said that over time his positions were the same and they were repetitive and that he'd learned what he was doing for the most part on the job. Throughout our relationship he'd often told me that he resented his brother and that was why he never introduced us when he visited Mark on rare occasions. I had never met him. It was clear he felt entitled to take his brother's hard work and apply it to himself and I saw that he wasn't remorseful and shrugged at it. Too many unsettling things had been happening and were being revealed at once and because of it I could finally see there were too many incidents and patterns to dismiss. I was constantly being made to feel badly for him as awful things were spaced apart and he'd always readily lie and deny but I could finally see he was a terrible person and I was leaving. After talking he fell asleep and I immediately took his phone into the bathroom to look for clues into his behavior. Inside was dozens of women's phone numbers, text messages, emails and their pornographic photos. He was addicted to sex and a serial cheater, it had gone on the duration that I'd known him. He was carrying on with several women, some of them had the same name and it appeared there was more than one coworker in his personal life. I was beyond grief stricken to see that he had been carrying on an affair with my friend Elizabeth, I wanted to throw up but I was in too much shock. I saw their text messages and her nudes and I knew she could easily frequent seeing him. I didn't spend all week with him and they worked across the street from each other, both of their job sites were only one mile from Mark's residence. The pain from seeing that they had been carrying on was so profound that I shut down and went into denial about it. I couldn't handle another knife being driven in my back. Who the hell could I trust anymore? I quickly gathered the few things I had in his closet and when I removed my clothing from the hangers, someone had sprayed perfume on my things and had hung their cheap and tattered underwear underneath my clothes so that I'd find them. I knew they didn't belong to Laura or Elizabeth because they wouldn't fit and they were from a store that teenage girls frequently shop. It seemed obvious that they belonged to the young woman who often visited her male friend that lived upstairs from Mark. He'd moved in only a few weeks ago and they'd invited us over to a party they'd just had. This young red headed woman Ashley had been drinking and when the party disbanded at the end of the night I had quickly went to use the bathroom. When I had come out I was looking for Mark and when I asked where he'd went the host nervously looked in the direction of his walk-in closet and when I opened the door I found them inside. She had gotten very friendly with Mark and was on her knees and had her hands on his belt buckle when I opened the door. That night didn't end on a high note and after I reacted, Mark pinned me down and pulled my arms behind my back and sat with one knee on them with his other knee on the side of my neck. He wouldn't release me but I wouldn't stop screaming and afterward he threw a tantrum and said that I had created problems for him and his neighbor over nothing. I knew it wasn't true but he was starting to really frighten me so I didn't continue to press it. Given how comfortable Ashley seemed to be with him I knew these things belonged to her. The toxic behavior was more of the same with Mark over and again. He'd used and manipulated me for so long but the saddest part of it all was that I had allowed it. I couldn't even begin to understand how I could let it go on for so long. While I continued to remove my belongings from the closet I saw he had Viagra bottles and some other drug that looked like cocaine wrapped in his clothes on one of the shelves. The events that were unfolding were so disturbing it was like navigating a minefield, just as our entire relationship had been. I said a few choice words to him while he laid there with his eyes closed, too scared to face me and the truth. I threw his phone and the cheap undergarments at him and walked out. He continued to reach out to me many times and left messages over several weeks to say that he was sorry that my clothes had been ruined and that he loved me, but I had found the strength to finally leave and I wasn't going to be drawn back in. He had conned me for the final time and his behavior was so outlandish and so were his lies, I had to change my number so that I wouldn't hear from him anymore. I learned later that he didn't follow through with securing the restraining order against Laura and that she had filed and secured a domestic violence protection order against him several weeks after I had last seen him. Mark always portrayed himself to be either a hero or a victim, but never the villain.

I did see Elizabeth a handful of times over the course of a year after I left Mark. I didn't confront her about what I'd known for a variety of reasons but mainly it was because I felt as though we were family. I was hurt but I'd frequently given many chances to my siblings and looked past their terrible behavior for the sake of them being family and I placed her in the same context. I was also very close to her daughter and she had gone through some difficult and dark moments in her life and she looked to me as an Aunt. She came to me for advice when she couldn't confide in her mother; I was surprised that Elizabeth could be so callous when I had been a very loving friend to her and her family. However, I had long known the truth of who she was. I knew that she lived a double life for most of her marriage with one of her co-workers and that she also carried on with some of the men that regularly sat at her dinner table with their wives. Even though I knew all of this, I'd known her for many years and she knew what Mark had put me through with the lawsuit. There were so many layers to the grief of her disloyalty that I couldn't immediately face it. She continued to ask about him each time I'd seen her and I recognized they were still in contact and we had a falling out. I didn't have the heart to tell her husband what I knew because it would have devastated their family. I'd once again put others before me and carried the burden of what she'd done to me and who she was, meanwhile I was devastated. The emotional upset lingered for a very long time and it added to the list of deceptions that chipped away at me. I started to recognize that the more chances I gave to those that hurt me, the less they respected me.

I'd let terrible people into my life from lack of boundaries and things needed to change but I didn't know where to begin. Recovering from the fallout of knowing him felt hopeless, there was so much destruction and everything about my life, physical/mental health, career, and finances were ruined. I never even loved Mark, how could I allow this to happen to me and for it to go on for so long? I started opening up and talking in detail about the events of our relationship with my psychiatrist. I'd been going to these appointments for three years and hadn't discussed Mark at all. After I'd allowed him to move in there had been many stressors and so many traumas that had happened all at once and coincided with the headache of being served a lawsuit and then many countless other things afterward. I knew he was harming me and that he continued to do it and yet he'd always get me to feeling badly for him and I allowed it to continue. I had absorbed the blame and felt like I had taken a huge fall in life when I had been found guilty and held half responsible for his misdeeds. I was living with tremendous guilt from having an abortion and I didn't care what happened to me, I felt despicable. I made excuses for him afterward because I felt humiliated by his behavior and senseless to have allowed him in my life in the first place. Dr. K sat there over a few sessions and listened to the many traumatic experiences I lived through while I knew Mark, about my fears during the economy crash and my general feelings about myself and some other past traumas. I was completely done with him but it felt like I was going through aftershocks and that I had many years' worth remaining from the fall out of knowing him and I didn't know where to begin to fix it. Dr. K mentioned Stockholm syndrome is a coping mechanism through terribly frightening situations but I didn't want to listen any further. I'd heard about it but I didn't think it applied to me at all and besides, I knew Mark before life really fell apart. I decided that I didn't want to ever talk about him again. If this were true, it seemed I maybe should have been more forthcoming as to why I had started seeing Dr. K at the start but he'd only asked about my symptoms of my nervous breakdown and not the events that led up to it. During that initial appointment I'd mentioned rather sarcastically that certain family continued saying I was bipolar over the years because I had angry moments in my life, depression and mood swings; and he'd diagnosed it. He had the pill packs at the ready to begin taking at his office and I didn't question it because we have other mental illness in the family. But a mental disorder and a coping mechanism aren't the same thing. That first appointment was so long ago; all I wanted was more pills.

23

DEAD END

I had tried to process my emotions from all of the events that took place but I couldn't. I stayed numb to everything no matter how hard I tried to process what had happened. I didn't cry over him or over anything that had gone on, I just pushed the thoughts of him out of my mind. I was still taking my cocktail of prescriptions and they were continuing to keep my emotions dulled down but life didn't stop and I did my best to move on.

Several months later JD contacted me again and he said he wanted to see me. He'd told me that he was single now and that he bought a new home but I wasn't sure if I wanted to meet with him. So many years had passed and life had really gone downhill for me. I had lost all confidence in myself and I knew I was nothing like he remembered. It had been ten years since we had first dated and he stayed infatuated with my ghost of a distant time gone by. I was reluctant to go but he was persistent and I decided to see him. I was still frightened about driving at night and tried to get him to meet during the day but he insisted on seeing me in that moment and I drove in a state of panic to meet with him as I navigated my way to a midpoint. We chatted for a long while and spent the night together but afterward he shunned me and didn't want anything to do with me. We met again a week later and he told me that he was still married. I was livid, and I was broken hearted over how he'd treated me. He came back in to my life at a low point when I could've used a friend, but he had ulterior motives. He'd told me that night that his ex-wife was practically engaged but it was clear from how things played out after we spent the night together that he just used me to rub into her face. It felt as though he drove a knife in my back and delivered the final kick to relish in watching me fall. I was crushed but I had made the right choice in walking away from him many years ago. He was no different than the other predators in my past and I never wanted to speak to or hear from him again.

In an extraordinary sequence of events within just days before hearing from JD, I had seen a woman in my small isolated town that he and I both worked with many years ago. When I saw him I'd mentioned to him that I had seen her while I was out buying cigarettes. Katy walked by me in the small cigarette store and she looked at me but I could see she wasn't sure who I was because I had drastically changed in appearance. She and I had once been personal friends while we worked together, I had met her at work and we had the same job. I had been to her home several times and we'd gone out to the local night clubs together to go dancing; and she had a very abusive boyfriend that she'd been with for many years since she was a teen. He controlled her and I couldn't understand how because I could see that he needed her more than she needed him. She was very smart, reliable and made good money, kept her house nice, had a nice car and took care of her responsibilities. His abuse had taken a toll on her and she was infrequently using recreational drugs to cope and escape before tragedy struck. I'd only met him two-three times but I never wanted to be in the same room with him because he gave me a bad feeling but in large part I knew how he treated her and didn't want to know him. He was horrible to her and I wouldn't visit with her if he was home. In a drug fueled rage one night he tried to kill her and landed in prison for it. Very soon afterward she had gotten extremely lost in life and I couldn't be friends with her anymore and we parted ways. She looked herself again when I saw her at the cigarette shop and I was curious to know if her boyfriend had gotten out of prison. I was shocked to find the news online that he had killed himself while still incarcerated when he was presented with evidence that tied him to the murder of my classmate at Granada High School, Jessica McHenry. I hadn't been paying attention to the media when that news originally broke and it was years old now. When I read that I remembered that Katy took me to a party one evening in Livermore and I met Ilene Misheloff's brother there, she had introduced us. I made the poor guy uncomfortable when I started asking questions about his sister who had been missing for years. I haven't seen or spoken with Katy since the day we parted ways many years ago but what an extraordinary coincidence and in seeing her only days before I heard from and saw JD.

A year after I'd seen JD, my life was moving along and life started to look up. I had bought a fixer-upper home near my parents and started to taper off of my medications. I had withdrawals that wouldn't go away but after a while I noticed that I was coming back into a feeling of being more like myself and I had drive again. I started a business that I had to commute long hours to and from each day and I was feeling good and proud of myself. I would never have been able to accomplish that if I was still heavily medicated or with Mark. My doctor said that this drive was grandiose energy created by a manic phase, but I knew that it wasn't true because I had always been ambitious. I was so tired of everyone dragging me down and keeping me suppressed - I started to push back and told him I wanted off of the prescriptions but he insisted that I needed to be on them for life. I was experiencing withdrawal symptoms every day and it was difficult to push through with this feeling of being zapped every waking minute. However, I had also lost a significant amount of weight once I drastically reduced the dosage of the meds. I started feeling exhausted from working so hard and was gone many long hours each day; and the zapping pain in my head would not stop. I had to work hard to keep from being irritable due to the pain and I pushed myself very hard to accomplish these new changes in my life; and they kept my mind off of what had happened in my past. I'd carved out a new life but only months after I opened for business I had gotten ill from burnout, and had to shut down. I had business credit open and without making sales at my store I was financially imploding quickly and having a hard time paying my bills. My new car was repossessed and I was stuck living in a small isolated town without Uber or taxi service. The happiness that I had started to feel with accomplishing these life goals after years of feeling void and suppressed quickly waned and was replaced with worry and angst. I felt so stuck with no way out of my predicament and went on assistance so that I could afford to keep my home. I was living a completely different existence and I was so far in debt with no way out. I couldn't find employment after the lawsuit and I'd risked the little money I had left by going into business for myself and now I was also drowning in that debt. Life was going back downward and I was tired of fighting to get ahead and I gave in to the notion that this was all there was meant to be for my life and contemplated suicide many times. What had become of my life? It wasn't supposed to be this way I thought over and again. My thoughts ruminated and I kept thinking that if only if could reverse time, I would do so many things differently. I was isolated and fell into a severe depression and stayed in bed for the better part of a year. I started taking all of my prescriptions again at full dose and the zaps went away immediately within hours; and the weight piled back on just as quickly too. I thought to myself every day - *if I could only go back to a point when things weren't too far out of control in life, I would change it all. I would make better choices in every area of my life.* I laid there and thought of all the many ways and things that I would do differently if only I could rewind time and start over. One night while I lay there I came across an article about a woman that had gone viral as a new beauty guru and I reached out to her. She promoted my products and it forced me to focus my attention back on my business and get familiar with online sales very quickly. My brand garnered national attention while I was in one of the deepest depressions of my life and I started feeling better and hopeful again.

I had my lash business to focus on and my milestone 40th birthday was fast approaching. My parents lived close by but my sister was having some life difficulties and we were all grieving the fallout of her choices. We didn't speak with each other regularly while we were trying to cope. Each of us was going through our own difficulties and also suffering from life's problems. I didn't want my birthday to pass without doing something to celebrate and I was feeling happier now that my business was turning around for the better. I went online to a dating site and met Mike. After the rape I didn't think anyone would believe me so I didn't tell anyone and I didn't report it. I just kept thinking over and again, *who would believe me?* I was there in his home and was ready to engage in having sex with him after our date until he started hitting and choking me. I knew once he had hit me that it was about power and control and that he wanted me to feel fear and pain. I felt certain that he had found the lawsuit information online and took advantage of me. Given with what I had been through and how I was now living, my life had turned out horribly and Mike was a business man in his community. Who would believe me? I was humiliated by what he had done and I felt disgusting and I just wanted to wish it away as though it hadn't happened. I had borrowed my parents' car and when I sped out of Mike's driveway I drove home to my place in a state of shock. I instantly felt to blame for what happened to me. Several thoughts were swarming in my mind and I was coming apart. I just wanted to forget and wish it away and also wish me out of existence too; I didn't want to tell anyone. But the thoughts of what he'd done wouldn't stop and I began to think about how the others had used me as a scapegoat for their ill-gotten gains and had gotten away with it. They'd all taken advantage of me in ways I hadn't been capable of stopping and I had long ago been soul raped and had been broken. I felt like I was damaged goods, a throw away that no one would miss. I had lost my voice and resolve long ago; the capability of defending myself had been stripped of me. No one was going to help me, I thought. I hadn't even driven to Mike's place in my own car because I no longer had one. I stayed consumed in these thoughts and emotions and replayed the events of that night over and again in my mind. They wouldn't stop. I couldn't run away, not even with my pills. A week passed and I was still consumed with emotion and I was still bleeding and in pain, and my already fragile state of mind shattered. I had just fallen into the darkest days of my life and as I struggled to keep from being swallowed by the abyss, despair called out to me. It kept calling my name. I slipped further into the black hole with the tentacles of pure evil gripping me and pulling me down. I couldn't breathe, I was cracking. I wanted out from the pressure of the thoughts and haunting memories of everything that had gone wrong in my life. I tried to commit suicide.

I had several vials of different pills and I crushed all of them and washed them back with alcohol and in my inebriated state I stumbled around and I slipped in the bathroom and severely hit the back of my head. I could hear what sounded like an ocean current and felt a dulled pressure at the base of my head behind my right ear. The pills and alcohol kept me from feeling the pain from the crack in my skull. I could hardly move but I managed to get up and stumbled about and then tumbled down the stairwell. Darkness.

24

AWAKENING

I woke up naked and neatly tucked in bed upstairs as though I were placed there. I felt confused. For a fleeting moment I thought I had lived a life that resembled a horror movie; that I had taken so many destructive paths and made extremely terrible choices for myself. There were many people there that had hurt me along my journey and I felt alone and frightened and had been abused at various points in that life. I was emotionally and psychologically tortured too and I had become a drug addict of sorts from a bunch of pills that I didn't need. I was running from something but I couldn't go anywhere. I was far too trusting of people that smiled in my face but conspired behind my back to harm me; but I was persistent and they didn't like that. I kept moving forward so that I could find my way home but it felt like I had been caged and kept from reaching my destination. I had been blamed for some crazy bullshit that revolved around ton of money. I had treacherous friends and lovers in that life, including family members and complete strangers that hated me, took from me, did me harm and wanted to see me gone. I had been raped more than once in that life; and one of them times was as a little girl? Oh my goodness, how frightening! What the fuck? I'd finally cracked and come out of my mind and I had been left for dead! When I'd had enough I then dreamt that I shut my eyes and cried as I fell into hole and I kept saying over and over that all I wanted to do was go home and Grandma came to me in this dream. She was there to help me find my way back but I couldn't see her, I could feel her energy and knew it was her. There was something that looked like a bent T.V. screen that surrounded me and I was asked to look at my life and forget about all of the bad experiences and people. I was only looking at all of the wonderful moments and people in my life and I was asked if I wanted to see the future and what it looked like with me being happy. I said yes and I looked and could see a different life of freedom, love and fulfillment and I was smiling. I saw experiences I hadn't lived and people in my life that I hadn't met yet but I couldn't see the details of their faces. I was floating away and said that it was getting too dark to see. Someone was worried about the time. I heard them say, it's time, you're out of time and I kept hearing seven....seven...seven. I didn't know what it was but I wanted to go home now. I was ready. Grandma told me that I had something I had to finish and I had to go back for now. I had a purpose to fulfill and it had to do with the generations before me and those that came after and something else about helping. Look at the numbers and you'll understand; it's universal, I heard. I didn't understand what she meant and she'd said that I would know later. Life had gone terribly wrong in that dream. Thank goodness I'm safe and that I'm home now. What a fucking nightmare!

The surge of one of the most painful headaches of my existence brought me into reality. I didn't know how I got into my bed and I realized almost as quickly as I had awakened that all of those horrifying experiences hadn't been a dream, I had lived them. In a moment I knew that I had survived something I shouldn't have and that something greater than I had spared my life. I didn't grow up religious or spiritual but I immediately went into prayer and as tears sprang to my eyes I said out loud, *"Thank you for loving me, guiding me, blessing me, holding my hand. I believe in you now. Thank you for saving my life and keeping me alive. I promise that I'm going to do better, be better, and live better than I have before. And no matter what, I'm never going to give up on myself, ever again.*" I now say this prayer every day.

After slowly moving to sit up I saw that my phone was neatly placed next to me on the night table and when I looked at the time it was very early in the morning but I focused in on the date and saw that it showed that five days had past. I was going through a very intense experience that I didn't understand and I didn't seek immediate medical attention. I had this complete knowing that I was going to be alright because I was alive. I was also incapable of explaining what had happened and not ready to talk about why I had attempted to take my life but thoughts of various traumas that had transpired didn't feel heavy anymore. I touched the back of my head and I could feel a very painful dent in my skull and couldn't put any pressure on it but there was no blood and no open wound. I knew with absolute certainty that I would be ok and that I was going to heal. I had to use the restroom and walked very slowly and held onto the walls to steady myself. I had other pets now and they were with me in my bedroom and were visibly shaking.

I was dizzy and vomiting for a few days, the pressure in my head was tremendous and I had to stay in bed to keep from falling over when I stood up. I had this strong inclination come over me through intuitive guidance on how to begin healing myself and to also begin meditating even though I had never tried to before. My head was in a lot of pain and I placed a light therapy device that I had onto my skull to help speed the healing. I did an online search for the meditative guidance and found many free recordings on YouTube and I picked one at random. I lay down and listened to the sound of a soothing soft voice with gentle music notes in the background instruct me to follow along with visualization techniques while breathing deeply and slowly. The voice asked that I keep my eyes closed and to move my eyes toward the middle of my forehead as I lay there breathing deeply and feeling relaxed. There are no true words for the experience, but the best way I can describe it is that I immediately went into a dream state but I was awake and felt as if I were floating. I wasn't physically floating but it felt that way and I could feel a vibrating current running through my body and it felt like electricity; like an electrical current that stayed mostly in the center of my body but I could feel it throughout. I didn't have anything to compare this to since I hadn't meditated before and I continued to follow along with the voice on the recording asking me to do a body scan. They instructed for me to check for any areas starting at the top of my head and through various points in my body that needed healing. I could feel the throbbing pain in my head, which was an obvious area. As my eyes stay closed I saw a bright green pulsating light appear in my forehead area and I began to feel a dull aching sensation in the area of my heart. I kept seeing this green light and having this inner call that repeated "seven". I instinctively knew it represented a reset of the seven main energy centers in the body. I also instinctively knew that the green light represented the heart area where it held love, compassion and forgiveness. I had insight that I needed to heal many emotional wounds that came from many events over the course of my life and several events that were highlighted which I have written about in this book. These events caused a misalignment in my energy field that blocked love from flowing to me and from me as well as caused a block in many of the other energy areas as well. I had been living with a broken heart from a broken spirit for most of my life and I acknowledged that it was being realigned and I was going to start with a clean slate so to speak. I had to work to do to complete the healing and afterward the emotional wounds would close off. In time I would grow from the healing and from that I would be released from heavy repeated life cycles, they were coming to a completion.

I continued meditating every day and on some days for several hours and I began asking myself questions about my life in the past, present and future and realized that I held the answers to everything I wanted to know about my existence. I could "see" a recall of all life experiences and they had stayed within my brain like a sponge. As I silenced my mind and got into a place of center and calm, I could extract information from every year of my existence with many details. Everything I'd read, listened to, felt, smelled, experienced, people I met - was stored in my memory. In a conscious state of mind I had forgotten so many experiences and people but it was never gone, it was buried in my subconscious and the information went back to the moment of birth. We all have this capability. Suddenly I knew why I lived the way that I did and I understood why I made certain choices for myself and why I allowed certain types people in my life, as an example to name a few. Many life experiences had left me feeling unworthy of love. I needed to heal inner child wounds and nurture myself and I hadn't realized that self-love had been missing or why. Through these meditation sessions the answers to all of my life's questions including my purpose became clear and I also began to understand the power of the heart. Over time when I learned what was at the core of my behavioral patterns I then learned to forgive myself for all of the terrible choices that I had contributed to that were detrimental to my life; and I was then able to feel compassion and forgiveness for those that had harmed me. As I progressed in my healing I was able to forgive, not excuse, but forgive and I set myself free from the chains of my past and I no longer felt stuck.

What I've learned is that trauma stays stuck in the body if it isn't healed it will manifest itself later in a variety of detrimental ways – both physically and mentally and it stays imprinted in your DNA and can be passed down into the generations. It can still be healed even if all seems hopeless, through behavioral changes and perspective. The emotional rejection and fear that I felt during my formative years from my father, coupled with the assault by my neighbor as a child, and the abuse I endured by my brother throughout my life - contributed to making me feel shame and unworthy of love. Even though mom and grandma aren't related, I'd also seen as a child how both of them lacked support systems in their lives. I also knew they had suffered their own traumas in life and it changed them. Some of their behavioral traits were very similar and had been passed to their children and I gravitated towards others that served like a mirror to my negative childhood experiences and I followed a pattern in life of self-destruction and people pleasing and stayed in an endless cycle of being hurt, rejected and used. I'd spent so many years in search of love and validation outside of myself and hadn't realized that I had been missing that or that I held the healing power of the heart within all along.

I went through what is known as a Kundalini awakening the night I attempted suicide and when I awakened and went through a process of healing, it was like a rebirth. I had a very close call with death and it woke me up to life. As I began healing and teaching myself a new way to exist, I recognized that I was still making mistakes based on habits but I was suddenly very mindful of that and I could then easily make different choices when I gained clarity on how they negatively impacted my life. My mind, body and spirit connection had been reset and I was guided on how to self-heal my physical health and my emotional wellbeing and bring forth self-love through mindful living, practicing gratitude and forgiveness; keeping hope and compassion alive, meditation, breath work, exercise, eating nutrient rich organic foods because they offer a naturally high vibrational state, drinking a lot of filtered and clean water, and eating a variety of cleansing herbs and vitamins to heal and nourish my internal organs, bones and mental health, including brain retrainment. I found free online meditation guides through YouTube including binaural beats that you can fall asleep to and your subconscious absorbs these notes. These are frequency sounds that retrain the way that you think and feel and how to live a more positive existence and reshape the thinking patterns of your life. Think in terms of how a plant can come alive to the sound of music or when day light comes and the world of nature and its inhabitants comes alive and you'll understand the concept is the same. As I surrendered to this healing journey and did all of these items they worked synergistically to help me set the course of events of my life in a new direction. I went through a rapid healing succession that I didn't think was possible because I had been so stuck in life for many years and the regular tools that I had grown accustomed to get me on track with life such as therapy and medication all seemed to stop working for me long ago. All of my senses have dramatically improved and I started to notice that I could literally smell the flowers from blocks away, my eye sight sharpened, my hearing became very acute, life was in vivid color as the veil of fog lifted and evaporated. I also developed a heightened awareness and very strong intuitive abilities that help guide my life. I stopped all of my medications and the withdrawals stayed with me for two years but I kept hope that one day they would go away and as I tried various ways to nourish my health, they did. This new found set of skills and knowledge changed everything around and the guidance on how to self-heal had come from within. I felt lighter in spirit and in time I no longer ruminated on the past and didn't have emotional attachment to any of the terrible experiences from the past anymore. I could see them for what they were – life lessons. Some of them were harsh and terrible but I finally understood the meaning in them and what life was teaching me.

I know from my experience that we all have the ability to self-heal but we haven't been given the tools on how and that is a part of my life purpose. It's important for me to share with you my knowledge and experiences to provide inspiration for change and give hope to those that need it. You can do anything you want in this life; you can change most anything but it all starts with the decision to stay committed to change.

I learned that the hurt and blame that we feel in life after we have been harmed and wronged comes from a place of ego and the negative projected emotions and behaviors that we feel afterward come from a place of lack from within. While I was going through my healing, the realizations of how I contributed to my own demise came forward and it felt like hell. I went through a process called shadow work to face my demons and came to a place of acceptance for all of the wrongs that I contributed to in my life. It wasn't easy to face but I had to if I wanted to live differently and overhaul my life; I had to surrender and let go. There will always be times when someone or something harms you; it's the harsh reality of the world. At some point you have a responsibility and a duty to yourself to take control of your life and stop waiting for someone else to save you. The past is history and history is in the past and we hold the key to change it all, we simply must choose to unlock our potential and stay committed to the journey.

It took me two years of daily dedicated healing to restore my body and during this time I had went to a neurologist to look at my head because I was still suffering from slight pressure and headaches but I could feel the dent had mostly healed. Dr. Santos was alarmed and after looking into my eyes and touching my head, she said that I had a major concussion and a skull fracture and wanted me to go to the hospital. I went for a scan but I wasn't worried, I explained to her some of what had happened and that I was there to find out my progress and things were fine. She recommended a lot of rest but I had already come a long way; I knew that I was still healing and would continue to be alright by practicing my own techniques. I recognized after I saw her that I was extremely lucky to not have suffered from long term physical or motor impairments.

I had to fall apart and reach the point of nothing to appreciate my life and existence and I made it out of the darkness however, no one needs to get to the point of suicide to make changes. I worked hard to improve myself and I moved on from living in Valley Springs. While I was healing I learned to embrace the isolation and my time there; the peace and tranquility was exactly what I needed as I embarked on my journey of self-discovery. I had dreams of continuing to establish other businesses and I wanted to move. With the help of dad, he and I renovated my home and I sold it. I was recovering and nobody knew what had happened but everyone was aware that I was going through changes. They assumed it was a midlife crises and mom told me that I needed to give in to the reality of my life and accept it as it were. I couldn't do that. They thought I was nuts to sell my home and pursue my dreams when I kept failing. The events and destruction of my life had been repetitive for years and they had witnessed it all. Igniting the spark for change in my life hadn't happened because I had reached middle-age; it happened because after years of dealing with problems that I in fact resigned myself to accept, I was assaulted during a low point in my life and afterward nearly died from a willful suicide attempt. I was living a new appreciation for life because I'd survived; only they didn't know that, no one did. My newfound appreciation for life drives my determination. I had the willpower now to continue pursuing my dreams and I took a big risk in selling my home because I didn't know how life would play out, but I was resolute to try and I pushed all fear aside. I sold my home and I didn't have a car when I arrived in my new town and after I settled in my sister contacted me. I hadn't seen or heard from her in four years but she knew I had moved back to the East Bay Area and she wanted a place to stay. She's dealing with her own addictions and I tried to help but it quickly fell apart and added an enormous amount of stress into my life after I allowed her into my home. She has caused a tremendous amount of distress, destruction and chaos in many lives over several years. I won't enable her behavior and we remain estranged with no relationship left to mend. However, I didn't let this setback hinder me and I continued to move forward. I quickly re-established myself in business and I opened Microhair Aesthetics, a permanent cosmetics and hair loss solutions center, in Lafayette, CA. I had to shut down when the Covid-19 Pandemic hit globally and I quickly pivoted my business to online sales with skin care and hair care products that contain organic and natural ingredients. I had been suffering from many ailments including alopecia which was triggered from the years of anxiety and stress that I endured and I used the healing properties of meditation and exercise for stress management, organic living and nutrition and supplements to restore my health. I have recently launched my newest venture, Evolutionary Body System which offers transformative healing services and products and I created The Transformation Reset, a program to help other survivors self-heal from trauma so they can get on with their lives. All of these products and services are an embodiment of my healing journey and lifestyle. I enjoy spending time nurturing my businesses, creating others and giving guidance. After a lifetime of traumas; ten years after I had been entrapped in a conspiracy of fraud and found guilty of a crime I didn't commit; and nearly four years to the day of my sexual assault, I sat in my first board meeting as one of the board of directors with my local chamber of commerce where I contribute my guidance and business expertise.

Life isn't perfect and neither am I but I am grateful that I survived. There are still times that I make bad choices but I have a lot of experiences that have helped me to become more resilient. Sometimes when life gets overwhelming I take a pause and all I need to do is look back to see just how far I've come. I say my prayer and remind myself that life is meant to be lived in the present and looking ahead with excitement towards the future that has yet to unfold. I know that my suffering wasn't in vain; through my challenging experiences came wisdom, healing and the courage to share my story to inspire change and to help others like me who want to reclaim their life when all feels lost. I hope that you continue to follow along on my journey of healing and self-discovery.

CONCLUSION

I didn't grow up thinking that I had been abused or had grown up with an abusive home life. My parents have always been there for us in many ways and outside of the day with the buckle when I was nine, my dad did not hit or spank my sister or I again and very rarely yelled at us. I didn't know what rape was a child and couldn't explain what the neighbor had done to me because I lacked the knowledge and because I was scared of dad. I also couldn't explain for lack of understanding how to, that the teenage neighbor was raping the kids in the neighborhood. Afterward, I then endured living with my brothers' abusive and temperamental behavior. This had gone on virtually my entire childhood and throughout my teens and it also affected my sister, Gwen. I was scared from what the neighbor had done to me and I was unhappy with how my brother treated me in life but I didn't see my childhood as abusive or terrible because I did many activities with school and friends and many other fun family activities too. At home I was very close with mom, and dad had really changed too when he was home more after life got very out of hand with Adam. My parents made poor choices and didn't always know how to be the best but they did try to be and they recognized their mistakes while they were raising us and tried to implement changes. I could see it back then. I can't fault them for being flawed or fearful or for being unable provide what they couldn't or didn't know how to do. There were unique circumstances to their lives that most parents don't struggle with and I recognized that many years ago as I became an adult. Mom suffered a terrible childhood when she was orphaned and those memories stayed imprinted and changed how she felt about herself and how she raised us. She was much more passive and often timid in life but she is outgoing while dad is quieter and more controlling. Mom suffered a lot of various traumas throughout life and at times she has cracked under pressures without being understood. Mom is a survivor. She had intentionally started having a family as a teen to escape her environment and we were each born from her love for and with dad. Dad truly wasn't ready to be a father until my sister was born. He'd also had his own traumas in childhood and there was a disconnect between him and grandpa that I could see. While dad was in his twenties my sister was born and soon after that he'd lost grandma and who she was to him after her mental health crises was mishandled and the prescriptions changed her. Dad didn't show a lot of emotion and he was taught not to as a kid and in certain ways passed that along to us. Because he was the disciplinarian as we were young kids, it made us fear him and it caused a rift so we couldn't go to him to seek help, advice or guidance when we needed it. However, both of my parents did the best they could while juggling kids and dealing with the frustration of life starting as teenagers. They created a love between them that didn't look easy but has lasted a lifetime. We've talked a lot about my childhood and they reflect on those years and felt at a loss and didn't know how to change things. They also had very different parenting styles between all of us because of cultural norms and other varying factors as the years went by. They've been there and have done many wonderful things for all of us over the years and I was grateful for their support and a place to stay during my lawsuit. They watched helplessly as I came undone and it took an emotional toll on both of them. When my sister later fell apart too from her own life problems, they were once again distraught over the undoing in the family and have had a hard time recovering from the emotional pain. Mom and dad were grandparents while they were in their forties when Adam started his family; they have poured a lot of nurturing and love into all of their grandkids who look up to them. The grandkids are all grown now and they continue to view them with the same love and admiration that I once had for my grandparents.

I hadn't recognized my childhood as abusive and I couldn't identify my relationships as chaotic nor did I consider them to be domestic violence. I didn't recognize that traumatic experiences were abuse and that the scars showed in how someone carries themselves through their poor behavior; their physical deterioration, mental health suffering, or financial decline. I thought it meant visible scars such as bruising and broken bones from being hit and that it also had to be constant and not only sometimes. When I began to heal I had to surrender to the knowledge that these experiences in my life existed and they had names to them. I was also unaware of narcissistic abuse and it was eye opening when I researched and learned of how many people had gone through similar experiences in their family, friendships and intimate relationships; and how they also didn't realize they were victimized. Relationships with narcissists leave detrimental and lasting scars; there are hallmark traits to this type of abuse and the abusers. The fallout breaks you down over time, destroys lives, hopes, dreams, trust in self and others, careers, inner peace and faith in humanity and it happens very slowly and infiltrates your psyche without you realizing it until you've been completely dismantled and feel powerless to change it. It's so important to have strong boundaries and a strong sense of self and not seek external validation so that you can protect yourself. Recovery from all forms of trauma feels hopeless but you can do it by working to establish boundaries, identifying your own behaviors and traits that contribute or cause the cycle of destruction, removing negativity and toxic people from your life and implementing positive changes. This takes time to do but you can do it.

How does one go about setting boundaries and feeling confident when you feel so low? Unlearn negative thought patterns that keep you feeling unworthy. Catch yourself when you're doing that and replace those thoughts with positivity. For example say to yourself: yes I can do this, I am worthy, I am good enough, I love myself, I am powerful. It isn't easy to unlearn the negativity that you've absorbed and have allowed to repeat in your mind for so long; it takes work to change it. When you take proactive steps and make it a discipline, wonderful things will happen. When you begin to believe in yourself your confidence and power will come alive. Learn to love yourself and listen to your intuition, it will never guide you in the wrong direction when it comes to people and decisions. When you are practicing your healing, be selfish with your time and energy because not everyone is deserving of it and you. You'll make better choices and feel confidence in yourself and you'll have the knowledge from your experiences to stand up for yourself and set boundaries without feeling guilty.

I struggled for so long with pharmaceutical drugs, alcohol, smoking addiction, major weight fluctuations, mental health issues like anxiety, depression, suicide ideation and emotional dysregulation. I learned to change it around for myself by making a commitment to understanding how they developed and then I worked on addressing them. These areas are difficult for people to talk about because there are so many stigmas attached to them, especially family dynamics and mental health concerns. This makes people who are struggling too afraid to reach out for desperately needed help and the cycle of feeling alone in their problems and feeling misunderstood continues to eat away at them. People die every day from suicide because of feeling unable to cope with their lives and feel afraid to talk about what has gone wrong and some can't articulate well and there are others that can't afford therapy. It's essential that as a society we acknowledge that mental health is just as important as physical health and that it needs to become normalized to speak loudly and find ways of coping and healing without judgment. It's time to stop making people feel bad or shaming them for things that have happened to them. Or causing people to feel they must suffer in silence for fear of being ridiculed over things they couldn't, can't or don't know how to control. Did you know that an imbalanced diet and many nutrient deficiencies can contribute to creating mental health issues? Many do not and it goes unrealized that when you are nutrient deficient your mind and body are shutting down. You'll notice this in poor digestion, poor habits and ruminating thoughts. For example when your body is hungry but you are low on energy you'll naturally reach out for something but instead you'll find unhealthy ways of curbing your appetite that turn into bad habits because you are low in energy and don't have the stamina to put together a healthy meal. The lack of nutrients will cause sleeping disturbances and irrational thought patterns amongst many other things. By not loving and putting care into you, an endless cycle ensues. If you are then faced with traumas of any kind it takes a lot of energy and nutrients for your instincts to take over and go into survival mode; the symptoms from the lack of these proper nutrients then heightens and recovery from a mental health crisis is prolonged. I changed many things for the better with respect to my mental and physical health and these are a list of items I did to change my life: I overhauled my nutrition by switching to all organic food and added herbs, vitamins and supplements. I keep grains to a minimum because most of them are GMO products and they are not easily metabolized and create digestive issue for me. This trickles into the dairy and meats areas as well so I select grass fed and pasture raised products. It's important to understand that your gut is considered your second brain and directly communicates to your brain through your central nervous system. I also meditate every day and I wrote down questions and answers from these meditations to understand myself and my patterns. I realize my first experience with meditation is unique and that also getting centered is sometimes difficult for others when getting started, I recommend starting with 10 minutes and working up from there to what is comfortable for you. You can also begin by getting out in nature and planting your feet on soil or sand; sitting or standing there while enjoying the environment. Surround yourself with trees, plants or the ocean; we are connected to nature and it's soothing and healing. If you remove the negatives by changing your diet, removing toxic people and your bad habits, including what you watch and listen to, your mental health and life will greatly improve. I listened to binaural beats at night before bed and when I got used to listening to them I then I listened to them while I fell asleep at night. We absorb the frequency of these sounds in our subconscious that help to improve thinking patterns and that in turn can help guide you toward success and achieving your goals. You can find guided meditation sessions and binaural beats for free on YouTube and it's best to use headphones when listening. I began exercise by starting with walking then I worked my way up slowly into cardio and then later I added weight training. I drink water every morning at the start of my day and throughout to flush out negative energy that is attached to emotions and I keep caffeine limited by drinking organic decaf teas/coffee. If one is still suffering from depression after changes in diet, remember to get outside in the sunshine for Vitamin D because our bodies do not naturally manufacture it. You can also purchase a light therapy lamp for your home. You'll also naturally feel tired if you are exercising and this will regulate your sleep. Put away the electronics and turn off the T.V., it's best not to have one in your bedroom. I wake up with thoughts of mindful living, expressing gratitude and appreciation for life. When I did all of these things I saw a profound improvement in my health, habits, behavior, appearance, sense of self and life and I began to naturally attract better people and experiences; and I also felt a release to the emotions that were attached to my traumas. Life came alive and my potential went from stuck to limitless. I haven't had a depressive episode in four years, I no longer suffer from ruminating thoughts, mood swings, high anxiety and I quit smoking and have no cravings. I'm much calmer and at peace in life. I also stopped taking medications, I healed my body and lost nearly eighty pounds and kept it off without my focus being on weight loss. I focused purely on my health and healing. Start with one of these areas for yourself and make it a discipline; add one of these changes and then add the other and then another so that you don't feel so overwhelmed with getting started. It only takes 21 days for a discipline to take hold!

Life is very different today and I feel happy. I no longer feel negative or empty and I don't find it necessary to fill my time with activities or bad habits to escape. When I look back on my life now it's as if I see the terrible experiences from a third person perspective. I remember all of the people, negative experiences and the emotions that were once attached to them but I no longer feel them. I can identify that they happened but I no longer relate to them in anyway because life has completely changed now and everything feels lighter. Which illustrates a great point - to leave the past behind you must live for the present and look forward to tomorrow. The past is history and history is in the past, learn to let go. Let go of memories that hurt you and of people that are toxic. It's not easy but it's necessary to get to the next chapter in life. We must always seek out the answers to life's lessons and understand what it is teaching us so that we evolve and grow. Keep in mind that failure is a natural part of life and it is also a lesson in life that we must learn to embrace. Do not fear failure and then label yourself as such when it happens. Believe in yourself and learn from your mistakes and you will gain the knowledge on how to carry yourself forward. This practice creates courage and strength and helps you to face down life's adversities then they happen.

I used to live in the past and stay stuck in my thinking patterns, I felt so resentful for how my life had turned out and it kept me from moving forward and living life. I thought if I ever had the chance to change it all, I would do many things differently. It's interesting to see the patterns of my life and through meditation I saw similar patterns between myself and past friendships with people that represented a mirror being held up for me to view. They were a part of my life as lessons but at the time I couldn't see that and didn't know to look for the meanings. There are far too many to list but as an example, Elizabeth and I had met immediately after I stopped seeing JD. She was actively dating a married coworker and continued her life this way; we had become friends because we shared that in common even though we otherwise didn't live similar lives. This lesson was teaching where I lacked in morality, integrity and boundaries so that I would "see" that I needed to learn to love and respect myself. She served as a reminder to what I'd done with having a relationship with JD even after what I had been put through by Aadi. If I didn't learn to realign my lessons life would cycle again and I would self-sabotage while continuing on in another toxic relationship (as I did with Mark), I would then be completely surrounded by those that lacked in these areas also. Life would later show me in another painful lesson yet again because I still could not "see". Her betrayal was meant to sting so deeply because time had come to an end in my relationship with Mark and my friendship with her too; life was giving me another wakeup call so that I would correct what I was lacking to put an end to repetitive cycles of self-sabotage. If I had always shown up in life with these traits intact, toxic people wouldn't last in my life but I had deep wounds that began in childhood; I needed to remember them so that I could heal and change my behavior and patterns. As another example I saw many parallels between myself and in my friendship with Katy. Just as Graham had seen in me, I saw how Katy allowed herself to be controlled when she had so much going for herself and also that her choices and coping habits from that relationship also affected her friendships. I had recognized in her back then that she had vulnerabilities and that she didn't see that they made her appear insecure even though she seemingly had her life together. Like me, she too had a sibling that seemed to be treated much differently and highly favored over her. I didn't identify these at the time as reasons for why she allowed someone so abusive in her life because I didn't truly understand the dynamics of how she felt about herself. I know that I felt rejected and unworthy by my loved ones and it made me feel flawed. I know that in my relationships I didn't want to reject my partners for those same reasons when they showed their flaws but my vulnerabilities also left a door open for those that had wanted something from me in some way, to get inside and latch on. I was looking for validation and when they didn't let go but continued to need/take from me, I felt a false sense of love. Lessons on how to deal with my life had also shown up for me in patterns of tragedy during different points in time with life changing moments like breakups, discovering betrayal, moving, getting laid off, starting a new business and all while happening during more than one global crises. 9/11 and the 2008 economic meltdown shifted the energy in the world to fear and it was disastrous for everyone. I internalized a lot of that fear while also dealing with toxic relationships and it all proved catastrophic for me because I didn't have coping skills or the inner-strength when faced with so much strife at once. It was a vicious cycle on my part of continuously poor decisions that were compounded because I was looking for external love and safety by attempting to stay attached and be saved by people who weren't good for me and didn't care about me.

Life dealt another repeated lesson to learn from, when I was approached by a woman at a local Women in Business luncheon that attempted to take advantage of me during the COVID-19 Pandemic. Candyce said she had recently gone into business for herself and claimed to be the founder of a newly formed local non-profit organization. She was starting a book project with a group of women and that was the basis for why she had approached me and asked me to join them, this book was a project, a compilation of essays for her newly formed non-profit. She lives locally and had a .org email address extension and I assumed after looking at her business name online that she was legitimate. I hadn't followed through to verify the non-profit because the .org extensions have inherently been recognized for use by non-profits. However, I didn't know until later that only a few months before we had met, the .org extension was made available to the general public and anyone could now buy them for use. I realized it was a personal book and not a book project for a non-profit foundation as we had all been led to believe. The nature of the book was about trauma-to-healing, and I recognized she had swindled several vulnerable women out of their money during a pandemic and that she had targeted me for fraud. I didn't give her any money but when I pressed for transparency she was very evasive and we parted ways after she wrote back to me and stated that she was planning to form her non-profit after the release of her book. I immediately contacted the police and the FBI to file fraud reports. While I stayed focused on trying to pivot my businesses, Candyce embarked on a smear campaign filled with fabricated lies and worked over-time to convince others she knew including some of the ladies in the group, to begin harassing me as she deflected from taking responsibility for what she'd done. After everything I've been through in my life and worked to overcome and recover from, I won't allow anyone to take advantage of me. It was another incredible charade by someone with extreme behavior and ulterior motives. As I'd found out later, she and I hadn't met by chance at all. I had been specifically targeted by one of her friends whom was an ex of someone I had dated for a mere four weeks! These unknown women harbored some secret hate for me out of nothing more than being driven by sheer lack in their own lives. The entire situation was bizarre and a display of entitled narcissistic behavior at its finest. This time I had the experience to identify the deception and determination to no longer allow anyone else to take advantage of me again, especially those attached to fraud. The sequence of events with Candyce happened to also coincide with the start of the prison sentence for the CFO of Autonomy and it gave me the push to write this book and tell my story. I have lived through reverberating effects for years as people mistakenly assume I am a criminal and attached to fraud and/or think I'm a sitting duck they feel entitled to take from and harm. I've healed a great deal, learned so many lessons of life and it was time to share my story to help other victims find their voice too.

It's important to nurture your inner-strength so you have the courage and determination to face down adversity when it presents itself. I've long recognized that when people get called out for their bad behavior they like to deflect and create chaos or spin the circumstances to blame their victims, but I don't allow it. Keeping mute gives manipulative people, abusers and bullies the notion that they can continue harming you and others and get away with it. If standing up for myself deems me crazy, difficult, jealous, aggressive, bitchy or anything else in the eyes of a predator - so be it. Ultimately life acts like a mirror and provides so many chances to see and learn lessons, it's up to you to decide if you're ready to evolve or repeat. I've developed strong boundaries and this allows me to stop harmful patterns of seeking external validation and to disengage from entwining myself with others that still need to work on mending themselves.

When I was given a second chance to start over and do things differently, I took it and never looked back. You can start over at any age with anything because there are no timelines or limitations to life. There are only self-imposed restrictions or unnecessary worries of what others may think. It's your life to be lived so live your best life for you! Make a list of new goals and start ticking them off one by one. You want to lose weight? Check. Want to travel the world? Check. Improve your relationships? Start a new business or go back to school? Check, check, check. You are in control of where your life goes despite what may have happened to you so keep moving and believe that you can accomplish greatness and start doing. When it comes to relationships of any type, don't spend any length of time with someone that isn't good to you or for you. Release people from your life who are toxic, gossipy and complain or those that are unsupportive. Learn to take care of yourself, handle yourself with maturity and integrity and cultivate healthy self-standards and the negative people will fall out of your life and/or be repelled. Pay attention to red flags, trust your intuition and recognize that it isn't your job to change, parent or fix broken people. Sometimes it's best to simply live life and lead by example.

Keep in mind that there will always be someone out there that will judge you and stay committed to misunderstanding you. I refuse to allow myself to be defined by my traumas and at some point you can't give zero fucks about what other people think - you have to live your life on your terms. When you're down in life they'll say you're weak; if you show anger they'll say you're imbalanced, if you don't look or behave like everyone else they'll say you're different, if you change your hair color they'll say you're privileged; if you lose weight then it's not enough or it's too much. It goes on and on. Who cares what anybody else thinks? I've worked hard to overcome a lot of difficulty and I've learned to accept myself exactly as I am and for who I am and I'm so much happier for it. Learn to accept yourself and your differences and do not let the outside opinions of others shame you or change how you feel about yourself. You are unique, inside and out, and you are not meant to be a carbon copy of someone else! You live different experiences and behave differently. You have your own unique blueprint and your own special gifts to offer this world, embrace it. Remember that you are worthy of everything life has to offer and that you are enough by simply showing up in life as your authentic self.

I choose to be happy in my life and appreciate how hard I've worked to change it. There are times I struggle with always feeling happy, that's natural. If I'm having a really bad day, I simply look back at how far I've come and recognize the destruction that I overcame and left behind. I own my truths and everything about my life. I own my mistakes, my flaws and faults. I own that I created chaos and missed opportunities. I own that I made very poor choices and that they contributed to causing the misdirection of my life. I recognize that happiness comes from within and that my thoughts, patterns, behavior and how I view myself matters and that it dictates how others treat me. I continue learning and I dedicate my life to positive change and to helping others see their light by showing up as my authentic self. I didn't want to reach the end of my life without having answered two things for myself – have I lived in my life's purpose? Have I done enough to make a change in this world? I thankfully have more time now and I'm still working on it.

TEACH ME TO WHISPER

The future calls my name but the past calls me Violet
Out of time
The past is history and history is in the past
Out of time
You know why I like coffee, Red
Out of time
It's dark now
Out of time
Listen to the blue waves of the ocean. Can you hear my whisper?
It's time. You're out of time...
Out of time
...
Wake up, 7
It's 11:55
33333 heralds
...
I hear not a whisper
The trumpets
Phoenix is here...
Oh, the time!
5:55
Awakened now, Stardust
...
To teach the whisper, one must first see
What's in Emerald City?
All that shall set you free...

-Yolanda Trevino

WHAT'S IN EMERALD CITY?

WHAT'S IN EMERALD CITY?

YOLANDA TREVINO

CONNECT WITH ME

Linktr.ee/itsyolandatrevino

www.EvolutionaryBodySystem.com
www.iLushess.com
www.LightbodyPublishing.com
www.MicrohairAesthetics.com

On social media:
@evolutionarybodysystem
@ilushess
@itsyolandatrevino
@microhairaesthetics
@whatsinemeraldcity

SEXUAL VIOLENCE AND DOMESTIC ABUSE RESOURCES

If you or someone you know has been a victim of sexual assault, domestic abuse/violence or sex trafficking, there is help and hope. If you are in immediate danger, please contact 911 or your local emergency number. The following resources are available:

National Domestic Violence Hotline available 24/7:
Voice: 800-799-7233
TTY: 800-787-3224

National Human Trafficking Hotline:
Voice: 888-373-7888
TTY: 711

National Sexual Assault Hotline (RAINN):
Voice: 800-656-HOPE [4673]

Suicide Prevention Hotline:
800-273-8255

Crisis Text Hotline:
For text based help for your comfort and you safety with sexual assault, domestic violence, abuse, suicidal thoughts, depression, anxiety, bullying and more
Text HELLO to 741741 (in US or UK) 686868 in Canada

SOURCES

1. Miller, Camissa. Never a Victim: A course teaching self-defense. UCCS Student Newspaper The Scribe, December 4, 2018. https://scribe.uccs.edu/never-a-victim-a-course-teaching-self-defense/

2. KTAR News. *October is sexual assault and domestic violence awareness month.* Arizona Department of Health Services, October 8, 2020. https://ktar.com/story/3610422/october-is-sexual-and-domestic-violence-awareness-month/

3. Amnesty International. Indigenous Peoples. https://www.amnesty.org/en/what-we-do/indigenous-peoples/

4. Mullens, Robert. *Autonomy buys e-discovery firm Zantaz for $375M.* IDG News Service, July 5, 2007. https://www.computerworld.com/article/2542356/autonomy-buys-e-discovery-firm-zantaz-for--375m.html

5. Goldman, David. *HP Takes $8.8 billion writedown on Autonomy.* CNN Business, November 12, 2012. https://money.cnn.com/2012/11/20/technology/enterprise/hp-earnings/index.html

6. HP Complaint: https://www.cpmlegal.com/media/news/111_2012-12-19%20FINAL%20Complaint%20_HP_.pdf

7. Ciesielski, Jack T. *How Autonomy Fooled Hewlett-Packard.* Fortune, December 14, 2016.

https://fortune.com/2016/12/14/hewlett-packard-autonomy/

8. Reuters Staff. *Ex-Autonomy executive cuts deal with U.S. in HP fraud probe.* Reuters, November 30, 2017. https://www.reuters.com/article/us-hpe-autonomy-crime/ex-autonomy-executive-cuts-deal-with-u-s-in-hp-fraud-probe-idUSKBN1DU2U5

9. Stempel, Jonathan. *Ex-Autonomy CFO sentenced in U.S. to 5 years in prison over Hewlett-Packard fraud.* Reuters, May 13, 2019. https://www.reuters.com/article/us-hpe-autonomy-cfo/ex-autonomy-cfo-sentenced-in-u-s-to-5-years-prison-over-hewlett-packard-fraud-idUSKCN1SJ29H

10. Browning, Jonathan. *Mike Lynch gets extradition court date as HP waits for verdict.* Bloomberg Law, October 19, 2020. https://news.bloomberglaw.com/white-collar-and-criminal-law/mike-lynch-gets-extradition-court-date-as-hp-waits-for-verdict

11. Davies, Robert. *Hewlett-Packard wins civil fraud case against Mike Lynch over Autonomy sale.* The Guardian, January 28, 2022. https://www.theguardian.com/business/2022/jan/28/hewlett-packard-wins-civil-case-against-mike-lynch-over-autonomy-sale

12. Sexual Violence Resources. State of California Department of Justice. https://www.oag.ca.gov/sexual-violence-resources

www.ingramcontent.com/pod-product-compliance
Lightning Source LLC
Chambersburg PA
CBHW072151200426
43209CB00052B/1129